MW00366831

TABLE OF CONTENTS

Disclaimer

The information in this book is, in the opinion of the author, sound tactical advice. However, please take the information in this book with a healthy level of skepticism. Don't do something that doesn't make sense to you. Additionally, the author is not licensed to practice law in any jurisdiction. Before incorporating any information in this book into your life, you should consult a competent, licensed legal and/or tactical professional. This book is intended to compliment formal training with a firearms instructor - it does not replace it. Your training is not sufficient without personal range instruction from a competent, certified firearms instructor.

ISBN 978-1-61808-121-6

Printed in the United States of America

Cover design created by Ron Bell of AdVision Design Group
(www.advisiondesigngroup.com)

Illustration credits
Upper chest drawing ©iStockphoto.com/ ilbusca
Pelvic girdle drawing ©iStockphoto.com/ JFalcetti
Human brain drawing ©iStockphoto.com/ ChrisGorgio

White Feather Press

Reaffirming Faith in God, Family, and Country!

Books by Skip Coryell

We Hold These Truths
Bond of Unseen Blood
Church and State
Blood in the Streets
Laughter and Tears
RKBA: Defending the Right to Keep and Bear Arms
Stalking Natalie
The God Virus
The Shadow Militia
The Saracen Tide
Civilian Combat: The Concealed Carry Book

Dedication

I dedicate this book to my wife and children ... the reason I train and carry.

Acknowledgements and Thanks

I can't possibly mention everyone who has taught me by name, so I'll just mention a few.

Rob Pincus of ICE Training, Massad Ayoob, Dave Spaulding, Bob Houzenga, Kathy Jackson and Andy Kemp for all their wonderful training, writings and videos.

Tim Schmidt and the entire United States Concealed Carry Association.

The National Rifle Association

Joel Fulton, Brian Jeffs and Nathan Nephew for their careful review and comment.

Terry Johnson of Firearms Legal Protection.

Civilian Combat

Combat

The Concealed Carry Book

Skip

Coryell

From the Author

As I write these words, I'm sitting in my minivan on the backside of Oak Hill cemetery in my home town. At first glance that probably seems a bit morbid, but I often write here, simply because of the peace and quiet the dead have to offer. The dead don't bother me; it's the living that I worry about. As I look out across the hodge podge of headstones made of granite and marble, I can't help but wonder how many of these lives could have been saved if they'd only known how to defend themselves.

And that's why I write; that's why I teach. I co-host a syndicated radio talk show called Frontlines of Freedom. It's the number one talk show in the country for military veterans, and I always say in my armed American report "Never outsource your family's personal protection." I've never understood why people do that. I can understand why people hire a plumber or a landscaper, but trusting someone else, a total stranger, to protect myself, my wife and my kids? That's a sad mystery to me.

The number one job of a sheepdog is to protect the sheep, and there's a severe lack of protectors these days. Couple that with an overabundance of human sheep, and you get a crisis. There just aren't enough people out there who are trained, willing and able to protect our families in a world growing more frightening by the day.

Fear, uneasiness and the deepening sense that we are vulnerable is driving everyday people to get armed and get trained. This is the age of the sheepdog. And I revel in that. I teach concealed carry classes primarily in Michigan, and I often call my classes "Sheepdog 101." I tell my students they are just beginning a journey on the warrior's path, and the journey will take a lifetime. So you'd best get started as soon as possible. And they are … by the millions, all across the country.

But here's the problem. We live in an age where the gun has been vilified by the media and urban society for decades, and most of these new sheepdogs have little idea how to operate a gun, much less use it effectively in a life-or-death gunfight. Let me be clear from the start, I am not an expert in gunfighting. I am a firm believer that the best way to survive a gun fight is to avoid it. I carry my gun every day, and I've never had to use it. I know how to use it, and, if the situation arises, I will do what needs to be done. But my first choice is to stay vigilant, see the threat coming, and to get out of the way. I know that doesn't sound very masculine or exciting, especially for a Marine Corps veteran, but it is the best way to flourish. I don't want to get in a gun fight, so I go to extreme lengths to avoid them. And that's what I teach my students.

The reason we train, is so that we never have to fight. Of course, sometimes you can do everything right, and still end up at the wrong end of the muzzle. As my friend and excellent trainer Rob Pincus says in his writings. "Evil exists. Some day evil will visit you. Will you be prepared?" I live by that philosophy. I hope for the best, but I train for the worst. And I train my students to do the same.

In the pages of this book you will find wisdom and knowledge which place you on the warrior's path to begin your transition from sheep to sheepdog. However, there is no substitute for real-life training, and I highly encourage you to read the book, then seek out professional, competent instruction in the art of personal protection with a firearm.

Train hard, train often, and train safe.

Skip Coryell

PART I

MINDSET

"Let me get this straight: Running, crying, whimpering, and hiding under desks and pews? You mean to say that when an imbecile walks into a church, office, a day care center, or school, stumbling about, almost zombie-like, with gun-filled hands at his side, blabbering incoherently to his next victim, the reaction of grown men and women is to run, cry, whimper, and hide under a desk or pew? The sheeping of America is nearly complete."

— Ted Nugent —

Chapter 1

In this chapter you will learn the following:

- The definition of civilian combat and how it pertains to the concealed pistol carrier.
- The serious nature of civilian combat.
- The importance of situational awareness.
- The role of law enforcement in civilian combat.
- The extreme personal nature of deadly force training.

(Taken from dictionary.com)
civilian [si-vil-yuh n] – noun
1. a person who is not on active duty with a military, naval, police, or fire fighting organization.

combat [n. kom-bat] – noun
3. Military. active, armed fighting with enemy forces.

1

What is Civilian Combat?

WHY IS THIS BOOK TITLED Civilian *Combat*? There are so many other things I could have called it … things less controversial, less prickly, easier on the ears. But … truth is, there's nothing warm and fuzzy about being shot with a gun or stabbed with a knife. The transition from civilian to combatant is huge, and very few people can do it with grace and ease. To the contrary, most people find it difficult, simply because they've been trained up and conditioned to believe that others will take care of them. Part of that stems from the urban culture we now live in, coupled with all modern amenities and technology we have at our disposal. We live in an instant society where everything we could possibly need or want is brought to us by simply pushing a few buttons. Need food? Pick up the iPhone and order some take-out. Want to watch the latest blockbuster movie? Order it on NetFlix.

But here's the problem. People have been conditioned to believe that law enforcement can and will protect them from all harm and wrong-doing. But the sad truth is they cannot. When you call nine-one-one, police officers are not instantly transported through your iPhone to your location where they handily and instantly dispatch the bad guys and save you and your family. Depending on where you are, the response time could be over thirty minutes. According to FBI crime statistics, the average fire fight lasts only three seconds, so if you're counting on the police to save you, you'll be sorely disappointed. While all good police officers want to help you survive in a deadly force situation, they cannot always be there, and they are not legally required to aid you. (Refer to the case "Warren Vs District of Columbia" for details.)

> **Learning to protect your family is intimate and personal**

The book is titled *Civilian Combat*, because that's the best description of what you'll be forced to do when you're attacked. In all likelihood you'll be fighting alone against one or more attackers who are stronger, faster, younger and more aggressive than you. When I was a kid, I used to watch an old TV show in black and white called *The Lone Ranger*. At the end of the show, the good guy (Clayton Moore) always rode in on his white horse named Silver and rescued the damsel in distress or the down-trodden farmer who was being threatened by evil. The music they played during the preamble to the show and also during the rescue scene was the *William*

Tell Overture and it just added to the excitement. But the truth of the matter is this: Evil exists, someday evil will visit your door. And when it does, the lone ranger will not be riding in on a white horse to save you, and you won't hear the *William Tell Overture* in the background. You are a civilian, but you are now locked in mortal combat. There is no cavalry. It's just you and whatever training, tools and mindset you brought along. You're on your own, because now, *you*, are the lone ranger. So, with that in mind, saddle up and let's get started.

> *"A fiery horse with the speed of light, a cloud of dust, and a hearty "Hi-yo, Silver, away!"*

Welcome to Class

AT THE BEGINNING OF EVERY CONCEALED CARRY CLASS I teach, I go around the room and I ask each person three things: What is your name? What is your favorite thing to do? and Why are you taking this class? I don't do this because I'm nosy. I do it for two specific reasons:

1) IT HELPS THE STUDENT BOND TO THE INSTRUCTOR. I've learned over the past fifteen years of teaching, that personal protection is, by definition, extremely personal. With well over 6,000 students under my belt, I've come to realize that it's natural for students to bond, in varying degrees, to the person who's teaching them how to protect their mates and their children from harm and death.

> When a civilian enters combat, he becomes a warrior.

It's not unusual for a total stranger to walk up to me and begin a conversation that goes something like this. "Oh, hey Skip! How's it going? It's been a long time. It's so good to see you again. What have you been up to?"

Almost always, this is a prior student of one of my concealed carry classes. I've become very good at nodding my head until I make the connection. But I always treat them as a friend, despite the fact I can't remember their name, because I know that on one special point in time we spent a day together on the range. And there's something incredibly bonding about shooting. I stood behind them, and to one side, as they began that most intimate of journeys, down the warrior's path, as they transitioned from sheep to sheepdog. Shooting firearms for personal protection is a growth experience, an American rite of passage, and, the very act of standing beside someone holding a deadly weapon ... is the supreme act of faith and trust. I trust they won't shoot me, and they trust that I'll do my best to protect them against their own inexperience and that I'll teach them what they need to know to prevail in a life-or-death attack. Mutual trust and respect is the cornerstone of all the best relationships.

> The average fire fight lasts only 3 seconds.

2) AS A CONCEALED CARRY INSTRUCTOR, AT THAT MOMENT in time, for that day, I am the most important person in their lives, and I need to be reminded of that. I'm not important because I'm good, I'm important because I'm teaching them to protect the people who are paramount in their own lives.

After teaching the same class for over fifteen years, the

hundreds of repetitions can sometimes get to me. But I have to remember that even though I've said this same thing a thousand times before to others, this is the first and only time I'll say it to this particular group of individuals. And that, in itself, is special and personal, and can never be underestimated. I must always be at my best. I must always teach with the same fervor and excitement as I did when I first started teaching. Anything less is a disservice to my students. They trust me, and they depend on me to give them the best training available. And I always work to fulfill that realistic and necessary expectation. After all... this is life or death.

Things to Remember

1. The police cannot protect you at all times.

2. You are responsible for your own protection.

3. Civilians can and should be combatants.

4. Learning to protect yourself and your family is an intimate and bonding experience.

Chapter 2

In this chapter you will learn the following:

- The 3 types of people.
- How to carry yourself in public.
- All about the pecking order.

> *"I'm a sheepdog. I live to protect the flock and confront the wolf. If you have no capacity for violence then you are a healthy productive citizen, a sheep. If you have a capacity for violence and no empathy for your fellow citizens, then you have defined an aggressive sociopath, a wolf. But what if you have a capacity for violence, and a deep love for your fellow citizens? What do you have then? A sheepdog, a warrior, someone who is walking the hero's path. Someone who can walk into the heart of darkness, into the universal human phobia, and walk out unscathed."*
>
> —*LTC(RET) Dave Grossman, RANGER, Ph.D., author of "On Killing."*—

2

A Nation of Sheep

AMERICA ONCE STOOD FOR INDE-pendence, self sufficiency and a can-do attitude that caused every other nation to envy us. There was no doubt about it; they either hated America or loved America. Because of that we had friends who wanted to be like us, and enemies who wanted to destroy us. I'm not sure America is like that anymore. Fifty years ago, we were locked in a life-and-death struggle with the evil empire, the Soviet Union. They hated us. But that was okay, because they also respected us. We also respected them ... not for their ideology, but for their thousands of nukes. That mutual respect and fear was enough to keep the world safe from nuclear annihilation.

We no longer have that deterrence. Not in the world, and not even in our country or in the cities and towns in which we live. Respect for human life has eroded on a world scale. We have Islamic terrorism threatening world conquest, drug cartels taking over our borders, and race riots in our cities. And it's going to get worse.

Growing up in a rural neighborhood, we had something called "free-range parenting." It didn't have a fancy name back then, but that's basically what happened. During the summer, we'd do our chores in the morning, then take off for parts unknown to play with the neighbor kids. Sure, we got in minor trouble on a daily basis, but we sometimes got caught and paid the price for our adolescent sins. This kept us in check, and we seldom went over the edge.

> **The wolf kills without remorse.**

Fast-forward to today. I don't dare let my kids out of my sight. Not because I don't trust them (I don't) but because I don't trust society in general. Raising and protecting my children is the ultimate responsibility, and it belongs solely to my wife and I. Never outsource your personal protection, and never outsource the raising of your children, not to the government, not to the hood, and not even to a full-time baby-sitter. It's your job.

Retired Lieutenant Colonel Dave Grossman, a retired Army Ranger, is the world's foremost expert on the topic of killology. While I was interviewing Dave for *Frontlines of Freedom* radio a few months back, I asked the colonel "exactly what is killology?" Dave told me "Killology is the study of the legal use of deadly force; it is the legal taking of another human life." He went on

> **Look like sheep ... you'll be eaten by wolves.**

to tell me there's been tons of research done on serial killers, lunatics, etc. For some strange reason people are enamored with murderers; they want to know how they tick; why they kill; what caused them to deviate from the rest of the human race.

Frankly, I agree with Colonel Grossman when he says, and I paraphrase, "It's more important to know how to defend against the killers, than it is to know why they do what they do." People have been trying to figure out insanity and mental illness for centuries with little progress. I doubt, even in our current state of hubris, we'll be able to succeed where others have failed. Let's be blunt here. I'm not that smart, however, I am smart enough to know that one good way to stop a bad guy with a gun is to kill him or throw him in prison for the rest of his life. I have very little faith in the criminal justice system, and rehabilitation is a rarity. It has long been known that a small minority of the human race perpetrates a large majority of the violent crime.

> Most of personal protection has nothing to do with your gun.

Colonel Grossman calls these violent criminals "wolves," and the wolves usually continue to prey upon the sheep with impunity until someone stops them, many times with the aid of deadly force.

Sheep Anatomy

IN MY CLASSES, I OFTEN CALL UPON MOTHER NATURE TO aid me in my teaching. The wolf sits on the hill and he watches the caribou herd. What is he looking for? He is searching for an easy meal: the weak, the slow, the sick, the young, the old; thus, we get the saying "Look like sheep and you'll be eaten by wolves." So the moral of the story is "Don't look like a sheep."

And then I say, "I'm going to demonstrate two people walking through a parking lot. Person A walks like this:" I walk past the class with my head lowered, hands in my pockets, and my shoulders slouched. I never look around, and I appear to be lost in my own little world.

Person B walks like this. Then I walk past them a second time. I raise my shoulders up and back. I hold my head high and my head moves around, scanning the crowd. I make brief eye contact with people as I walk past them, and I may even nod my head in acknowledgement. My hands are at my sides or higher up on my torso. And then I ask this simple question: "Which person is going to get mugged?"

> When carrying a gun, be very polite.

Instinctively, they all know that person A is the victim, but they can't always articulate exactly why, because much of it is nonverbal. Let's go over it now, item by item.

Person A

1) Head down – This is a big no-no. You should always be alert, scanning your surroundings, looking for trouble. How many times have you seen people walking through a parking lot while texting on their electronic devices? I routinely see people walking through parking lots while their thumbs type away in earnest on their cell phones. These people obviously have no idea what is going on around them. This is an invitation to disaster. They could be hit by a moving car, and wolves are attracted to people who aren't looking at their surround-

ings. Former combat hero and army veteran Colonel David Hackworth (God rest his soul) had a saying "Stay alert – Stay alive!" I live by that one.

2) Hands in pockets – Always keep your hands up and ready, especially in public where threats might exist. Unless you can shoot lasers through your eyes, you'll need your hands to defend yourself. Hands buried deep inside your pockets is not an effective combat position. (Unless, of course, you have a pistol in each pocket.)

> **Walk with confidence and make brief eye contact.**

3) Slouching shoulders – In the Marine Corps they constantly told us to "Put some pride in the body!" If you don't respect yourself, then no one else will respect you either. And bad guys tend to attack what they don't respect. Stand up straight and walk tall. Always look confident, but not cocky.

4) No eye contact – People at the bottom of the pecking order don't like to make eye contact; it makes them feel uncomfortable. If you avoid eye contact, it makes you look weak and vulnerable. When someone walks passed you, look over and make brief eye contact with them, and then move on. What are you telling them in that brief moment as your eyes meet? I see you. I know you're there. I can pick you out of a police line-up. And I am not an easy target!

If you make the wrong type of eye contact, you can get yourself in trouble as well. Again, comparing this to the animal world, if you make eye contact and hold it, your stare can be perceived as an aggressive challenge. If you challenge the wrong person, you could be on the receiving end of a good thumping. The goal here is to deter would-be wolves and to make them feel uneasy and accountable. Always seek to de-escalate and avoid open conflict whenever possible. For example, you're walking down a crowded sidewalk, and you accidently brush shoulders with someone; they turn and swear at you. That's okay. No harm, no foul. Just politely apologize and attempt to move on. If they persist, be alert and watch their hands, but still attempt to disengage. When carrying a gun, you need to be the most polite person on the planet. Never get in a physical confrontation, or even a verbal argument for that matter. Verbal jousting sometimes escalates to physical contact. Once you're roll-ing around on the ground, things can quickly get out of hand. Always be aware of your gun and how to protect it. Be trained in pistol retention. This is a must. Once he goes for your gun, that's deadly force and one or both of you can die. If a younger, stronger, more aggressive assailant gets the best of you, then you have a classic

> Never engage a rude person. Always seek to de-escalate.

George Zimmerman situation, and you are forced to shoot him. And remember, George Zimmerman prevailed in the gun fight as well as in the court system, but his life since then has been negatively altered forever.

You can see that a lot of this is subjective and nonver-bal. That bothers some people, because they find it difficult to change things they've been doing without conscious thought for decades. Once you start carrying a gun for personal pro-tection, everything you do has to be well thought out and have a purpose. It's a whole new lifestyle.

Pecking order

TAKE FIVE DOGS WHO DON'T KNOW EACH OTHER, STICK them in a small kennel and leave for a few hours. When you come back, one dog will be sitting up on his haunches, surveying his kingdom. The other four will be slinking off in the background, and when they walk past the alpha dog, they'll lower their heads. What happened while you were gone? Someone got their ass kicked. They established the pecking order.

> The pecking order applies to humans as well as the animal kingdom.

Some people tell me in class that animals are different than people. There is no pecking order in humanity. Really? On Monday morning the boss calls a meeting. Before the meeting people filter in, sit down and begin to talk casually.

"So what did you do this weekend?"

"Oh, I took the kids to a movie."

"Was it good?"

"Oh, yeah. It was great!"

And then the owner of the company walks in. Everyone shuts up, takes out their pens, getting ready to take notes. That's a pecking order, but it's not always this civil. Out on the streets it gets more harsh. Kids who grow up in gangs quickly learn where they are in the order, and, if they make a mistake and challenge the wrong person; they can die.

Massad Ayoob once told me about a study done in federal prison where convicted armed robbers were placed in front of a television. They watched a video of people walking down the sidewalk and were asked one simple question: "Which of these people would you rob?"

In the video, the first several people to walk by were labeled as victims "Sure, I'd rob them." Then a small woman walked passed, and the convicted robber said:

"No, I wouldn't rob her."

"Why not?"

"I don't know. I just don't trust her."

The tape was started again. The next person to walk by was a man, and the robber physically recoiled from the television.

"No way! I'm not touching that guy!"

In real life, the woman was an undercover cop, and the man was an Army Ranger. But the big question is this: How did the robber know? The answer is simple. When you grow up on the street, you develop a keen sense of character. You have to know at any given time where you stand in the pecking order. Challenge the wrong person and you can die. In addition to that, over time, criminals become very good at their jobs. An important part of their job is to select the weakest victims. As you might imagine, after a hundred or so muggings, they can instinctively pick out the sheep from the herd.

> Subordinate personalities don't like to make eye contact.

Once after class a woman approached me to talk about situational awareness and pecking order. She was very shy, with head lowered and shoulders stooped. When she spoke her voice was soft and unsure. The conversation went something like this:

"Okay, I understand what you're saying about pecking order and not to look like a sheep and all that, but … what should someone do if they really are at the bottom of the pecking order?"

In my mind I thought, *Wow! You sure are at the bottom of the pecking order. What a sheep!* But I didn't say that aloud. Instead, I gave her some very simple advice. "Fake it until it's real." Force yourself to make eye contact when you're talking to someone. Practice walking with your head up and scanning for danger. Do all those things that a confident person would do without thinking about it, and, eventually, it will become a part of you. Sure, it takes time, for some people, maybe even years. But it will happen if you stick to it. This technique is called behavior modification.

I remember when I first joined the Marines. They sent me to Detroit for a physical. I had a pulse, could walk erect and was capable of human speech, so they took me. Then I signed some paperwork. Then I raised my right hand and swore an oath to protect and defend the Constitution of the United States of America. And after that "POOF!" I magically turned into a United States Marine! Does anyone believe that? No, of course not.

Soldiers aren't made in a day, and it took thirteen weeks for the military to turn me into a Marine. First they beat the crap out of me for six weeks. They exercised me beyond anything I'd ever done before. They took me to my breaking point and added ten percent. It was that act of being pushed physically and mentally beyond any-

> You don't have to stay a sheep. You can move up the food chain.

thing I'd ever known that put me on the path to becoming

a Marine. Then my drill instructors began to build me up, to instill pride, discipline and a warrior mindset. I gained confidence and it showed in the way I walked, talked and carried myself. That's called "military bearing."

It takes time, and it takes conscious effort. But now, you are a sheepdog, a civilian combatant. Take the time to modify your behavior, and, eventually, it will become a permanent part of you. Then you'll walk with confidence, with no forced thought process. It will come naturally, as a point of habit, resistant to fear, giving the opportunity for courage.

Things to Remember

1. There are 3 kinds of people: sheep, sheepdogs and wolves.

2. Look like a sheep and you'll be eaten by wolves.

3. Wolves recognize sheep instinctively.

4. A great deal of personal protection occurs in your mind. It's a lifestyle – a mindset.

5. With training and practice you can move up in the pecking order.

Helpful Resources

1. You can learn more about Lieutenant Colonel David Grossman at his website www.killology.com.

2. David Grossman's books can be found on Amazon. com:

   • "On Killing: The Psychological Cost of Learning to Kill in War and Society"
   • "On Combat, The Psychology and Physiology of Deadly Conflict in War and in Peace"
   • "Stop Teaching Our Kids to Kill"
   • "The Bulletproof Mind for Armed Citizens" (DVD set)

3. Take online training from Colonel Grossman at www.grossmanacademy.com.

Chapter 3

In this chapter you will learn the following:

- The fight or flight reflex
- The process for deciding when you are emotionally willing to use deadly force.
- The difference between cover and concealment.
- The technique of visualization.
- Practical ideas and tactics for handling deadly force encounters.

3

Almost Anyone Can Kill

EVERY ONCE IN A WHILE I RUN across a person who appears so good, so pious, so righteous, that they couldn't possibly hurt a fly, much less take another human life. Whenever that happens, I become highly skeptical. Under the right conditions, I believe that almost anyone can kill.

To illustrate the point, let me tell you about a student I once had. I was teaching a husband and wife in a private lesson on their farm in southwest Michigan. We were on the range behind their barn, shooting at targets up against an embankment. The woman was shooting a nice, 9 millimeter Glock, and she honestly could not hit the broad side of a barn from the inside.

Usually, I can watch someone shoot for a few minutes and have them make adjustments to bring them on paper or to tighten their group. But with this woman, I couldn't see anything she was doing consistently wrong and she didn't have a bullet group. She had good trigger control, good grip, follow through, breathing control; it all looked good. I tried everything I knew to get her on target, but it was no use. I couldn't find the problem. Her husband told me she was a good shot, and that she usually shot better than him, so he didn't understand the problem either. I questioned her some more, and she finally threw up her hands in frustration and said, "I don't even know why I'm doing this! I could never shoot anyone anyway. My husband made me take this class!"

At her remark, a light went off in my head, and I interjected. "What if someone was trying to kill you? Could you shoot someone then?" She said, "No! I couldn't kill someone to save my own life. I'd just go ahead and die!" I thought that was rather odd, but I could tell she was sincere, so I thought about it a second. Even though most people have an aversion to killing another human, I personally believe that there are very few people on this planet who would rather die than protect themselves. Most people who have taken the time to train and prepare for that life-or-death encounter, have a point where they will cross the line and take a life. But the problem is this: by definition, sheep don't plan or train; they are oblivious.

> It could take years to decide when you're capable of using deadly force.

Earlier in the day, this couple had introduced me to their baby girl, so I asked her, "How old is your daughter?"

"Nine months."

"Okay, let's use a little training technique called visualization."

She nodded her head impatiently.

"I'm going to describe a situation to you, and I'd like you to envision it in your mind as I talk. Okay, here's the scenario: You're at the gas station filling your tank. A man drives up and parks next to your car. He gets out, walks over, reaches through the open window of your car, removes your daughter from her car seat and puts her in his own car. He then starts to get into his car to drive away."

There was a horrified look on the young mother's face.

> Protect the children ... always protect the children.

"At that moment in time, could you take another human life?" Without hesitation, this good, pious Christian woman responded, "I would kill that son of a bitch!" I said, "Okay then, that target down there is the man who is stealing your daughter. Fire away."

She never missed the target for the rest of our session.

Under the right conditions, almost anyone can kill. It's not a question of how good a person you are. If you're in McDonald's Playland, and a man comes in and starts shooting kids, are you going to watch while he goes from child to child in Sandy Hook massacre fashion, or, are you going to spring into action? I submit that a good person would be unable to allow the death of innocent children. And, even if they did, because they were petrified by fear, they would be forced to live with the reality of that decision forever. It would haunt them the rest of their days.

Humans have been killing for millennia with no signs of letting up. Evil is a part of the natural condition of humanity. We are all capable of good, and we are all capable of evil.

But here's the rub: sometimes it takes people years to

decide if they have it within themselves to take another human life. For some it's easy, but for others it's a huge hurdle to surmount. If the average gun fight lasts only three seconds, you'll be unable to make a moral judgement in the time allotted. In three seconds, you'll be fortunate to draw your firearm and put multiple shots on target. When someone sticks a gun in your face it's too late to think about it.

> **You won't have time to make moral judgements in the heat of battle.**

Good people have a natural aversion to killing their fellow humans. It's supposed to be that way, and that's a good thing. By asking my students when they are willing to take another human life, and when they are not, I've discovered that very few people have thought it through to a conclusion. Most of them don't know, and this will cause you to freeze.

Think it through

THE TRAINING TECHNIQUE I USED EARLIER IN THE CHAPTER with the woman who couldn't take another human life is called "visualization." I frequently use this in class. I'll tell everyone to close their eyes and to let this scenario play out in their mind's eye.

> *You're down the road at your favorite gas station on your way to work. You're in the back of the store in front of the cooler selecting your favorite beverage when you hear a woman scream followed by a man yelling. You turn your head and see a large man holding a pistol which is pointed at*

the chest of the store clerk, a woman in her twenties.

"Give me the money! Open the till now!"

The young lady is flustered and she's frozen with fear. She is trying to obey, but her hands are shaking so badly that she is having trouble complying.

Here's your situation. You have your favorite pistol on one side and your cell phone on the other. The robber is twenty feet away and unaware of you. Step by step, with as much detail as possible, tell me what you're going to do.

Here is a list of a few of the answers I get.

1) BLANK LOOK OF TERROR. "I HAVE NO IDEA WHAT I would do."

Okay, I can work with honesty. But honesty alone isn't enough to keep you alive in a gunfight. You'll need a plan. Fill in the details. Chances are this person still hasn't decided when or if they are capable of taking another human life. The fact they are at my class tells me they are exploring the option, so that's a good first step.

> He has a gun. What are you going to do? Take your time. You have 0.5 seconds.

2) "I WOULD FIRST SET DOWN MY mocha Frappuccino, pull my gun and shoot him in the head."

Wow! That's a decisive action with little to no hesitation. But is it real, or is he or she just playing to the crowd?

Sometimes people are full of courage and bluster in the class room, but then fall to pieces in real life. Truth is no one knows for sure how they're going to respond in a life-or-death situation until it really happens. We can guess, we can wish, we can fantasize, we can suppose, but things happen physiologically and psychologically that we may not expect. Surprise in a gun fight is seldom a good thing. This person rarely knows what it takes to make a successful head shot at twenty feet while your hands are shaking.

Of course, there are exceptions to this, but they are usually people who've already experienced combat and use of deadly force. They are exceptions to the rule simply because they've already proven themselves in combat.

Ability trumps ego. Don't intervene if you can't succeed.

3) "I WOULD CRAWL INSIDE THE cooler and close the door behind me." The woman who said this was of retirement age, and, I thought she was joking at first. Then, a few hours later on the range, I realized why she'd said it. This woman had no idea how to shoot a handgun. She couldn't hit a house if she was standing in it. In her case, retreat was the best option, simply because her chances of prevailing in this scenario were not high. Her nature was timid, and she didn't possess the skill set to intervene in a life-or-death struggle. She was still a sheep. I'm reminded of the famous line spoken by Clint Eastwood in the movie *Magnum Force*; "A Man's got to know his limitations."

This woman knew her limitations, and this knowledge would have saved her life, in this scenario. However, not all scenarios allow you to retreat, so I challenged her to expand her knowledge and to improve her skill set, so she'd be better able to protect herself in a wider spectrum of threat scenarios.

> We live or die based on decisions we make.

4) "I WOULD TAKE OUT MY CELL phone and call nine-one-one." This is probably the most common answer I get. Perhaps because we've been conditioned to call the police when in danger. This is a noble gesture, and certainly something that should be done. But there's a right way and wrong way to do it. And there's a right time and a wrong time as well. Before you immediately go to the phone for help, first ascertain your chances of success. The bad guy is within twenty feet and could very well hear you talking to the police dispatcher. Once he knows you're there and on the phone, you're pretty much committed to either fight him or comply to his demands. And, if you've ever called nine-one-one, you understand that dispatchers are paid to gather as much information as possible. They'll be asking all kinds of questions, requiring you to speak clearly and articulately.

So there you have four answers from a host of answers I get in my classes. But that always begs the question: "Okay, what 'should' I do in that scenario?" Here's what I tell my students.

There are certain things you can do in this scenario regardless of whether or not you "intend" to intervene. Here they are:

1.   Draw your firearm. People sometimes ask me "Why draw the firearm first?" It's because the cell phone will give you protection in five to thirty minutes, but the gun protects you in one point five seconds. Number one priority at this point is staying alive. Yes, it's good to be a responsible citizen and to call the police, and after that to be a good witness and help the police do their job. But you can't do any of that if you're dead. First, you have to survive.

2.   *Move to cover.* Ideally, you should be moving to cover and drawing your handgun simultaneously. Time is crucial in a situation like this. Remember the famous quote by Benjamin Franklin? "Do not squander time for that is the stuff life is made of." If you can effectively do two things at once, then do it.

> Always seek out cover. True cover will stop a bullet.

This is probably a good time to talk about cover. In this scenario, cover is not the potato chip rack. News flash! Doritos will not stop a bullet! Most objects in a convenience store will hide you, but this is not cover; this is called concealment. Concealment is better than a kick in the butt with a frozen boot, but true cover is your goal. By cover I mean a stone pillar, wooden column, metal cabinets, or a door frame. How do you know for sure if something is true cover? In most cases you don't. But you do the best you can with what you have at hand. If you choose the stainless steel coffee maker; it probably won't completely stop the bullet, but maybe it will deform the bullet enough to limit penetration into your body. (Or maybe it will spray scalding coffee in your face.) When it comes to cover, there are few guarantees. We'll talk more about shooting from behind cover later in the book.

Important Safety Tip

Watch out for the tail gunner. Sometimes, in a robbery of

this nature, an accomplice will first come into the store and check things out. When it's safe, he'll text out to the robber "Come on in. No cops." At that point he acts as a lookout and watches the robber's back. If there are other shoppers in the store, don't let them get behind you or approach from the side. (We'll talk more about auditory exclusion and tunnel vision later.)

> Self defense scenarios change from moment to moment.

3.   *Call nine-one-one.* I say this with a caveat. Only call nine-one-one if you can safely do so. If you can't talk without being discovered, then just push nine-one-one and place the phone beside you. Dispatch will trace the call. Once they know the address, they'll send a cruiser by to investigate. Most cops recognize convenience stores as "Stop-n-Robs" so they'll approach with caution.

4.   *Monitor the situation.* At this point you go into monitor and assess mode. And the question you continually ask yourself is this: "Is this a routine robbery, or is he going to shoot the clerk?" In a 'routine' robbery, they take the money and run, but that's not always what happens. Sometimes the clerk gets shot. You are going to live or die based on decisions you make. The clerk is going to live or die based on your decisions, and so is the bad guy. So make very good decisions.

Important Safety Tip

This is also a good time to assess trajectory and penetration. Where is the bullet going to go if I have to shoot? Will

I hit the clerk or a bystander outside? Position yourself to minimize this danger if you can. Think about shot placement. Where do I want to aim? The angles may be changing from moment to moment.

Bear in mind that all self defense is scenario-based, and that all scenarios are extremely fluid and dynamic; they change from moment to moment. For example, if an unsuspecting cop walks through the door, the scenario has taken a drastic turn. Change even one small detail of the scenario and you change the outcome. This is no longer a 'routine' robbery. With a high level of certainty, we can conclude that a gunfight or physical altercation is going to occur. (This is an OODA loop moment that we'll discuss in detail later.)

> Self defense shooting is not black and white.

Do you intervene to protect the cop? That's up to you; it's a personal decision that only you can make. If you intervene is there a chance you could die? Absolutely. You might even get shot by the cop you're trying to protect. But life isn't fair – never has been and never will be. If you want fair, play Monopoly. Just do the best you can.

Most of my students want cut-and-dried answers; they want it to be black and white. So do I. But life isn't that way, and neither are self defense scenarios.

Students always ask about warning shots or challenge commands or shooting to wound. So here is my opinion.

Warning shots. From a purely tactical perspective, I advise against it. The bullet is going somewhere, and most times you don't know where that is. Sometimes warning shots can give the impression that the deadly threat was not imminent, that you had not yet reached the threshold of legal deadly force.

And firing a warning shot is, by definition, use of deadly force, whether you hit somebody or not.

Shooting to wound. Most of my students seem to get the bulk of their handgun knowledge from Hollywood. Students routinely ask the question "Wouldn't it be better to just shoot them in the knee?" In a word "No!" In two words "Hell no!" We'll talk more about that in a later chapter.

Challenge commands. Good people (most of the ones who take my class) possess a strong sense of fairness. From the playground we've been taught to fight fair. Not anymore. Only issue a challenge command when you are safely behind cover. Again, more on that later.

Things to Remember

1. During a gun fight you will not have time to decide when you are willing to use deadly force.

2. All of self defense is scenario based, and all scenarios change from moment to moment.

3. Protect the children, even if it means putting your own life at risk.

4. When deciding when to use deadly force, keep your ego out of it.

5. Warning shots and shooting to wound are both uses of deadly force.

6. When using deadly force, shoot to stop the threat.

Helpful Resources

1. One of the best things I've ever done (as someone who carries a gun for self defense) was to take a class taught by Massad Ayoob called *Judicious Use of Deadly Force*. The class was three days of intense classroom instruction on the nature of deadly force, when you are justified in using it, and what are the effects it will have on you. Massad Ayoob is widely considered to be the world's leading authority on use of deadly force. The class has since been renamed to *MAG 20/Classroom – Armed Citizens' Rules of Engagement*: You can register for this class by going to the Massad Ayoob Group website at: www.massadayoobgroup.com.

2. If you can't take the above course, at least read the book by Massad Ayoob titled *In the Gravest Extreme*. It is available on Amazon.com or anywhere else books are sold.

Chapter 4

In this chapter you will learn the following:

- Why you need advanced training.
- The type of training best suited for you.
- The importance of training under stress.
- Where to seek out quality training.

> "A gun is not a magic talisman whose mere presence will ward away evil."
>
> —*Massad Ayoob, International Trainer., author of "In The Gravest Extreme."*—

4

Anyone Can be Killed

MOST PEOPLE WHO COME TO MY basic concealed carry class are neophytes. That's a huge change from fifteen years ago when I first started training, and it's a good thing. Fifteen years ago my average class was composed of ninety percent middle-aged men who'd been hunting and shooting their entire lives. Fast-forward to today and you get a whole new clientele.

These days, half the people I teach have never touched a handgun more than a few times in their life. I see a lot more young people in their twenties coming to class, and that's refreshing since these kids are the future of our country. They are young and strong and fast, and I'm more than happy to teach them the skill set they'll need to protect themselves and their future families.

On the opposite end of the spectrum I have a large amount of retirement age folks as well, people who've gone sixty and seventy years without feeling the need to carry a gun who are now coming out in force to suddenly learn how to protect themselves with handguns. This is encouraging as well, because these are the folks who'll be targeted by society's wolves. They'll be perceived as slow and weak as the thugs and dregs of society pick out their next prey.

> **The gun is only as good as the person holding it.**

And then we have the fastest growing segment of the shooting sports: the ladies. Wow, do they ever change the personality of a class. They have special concerns and needs that have to be attended to as I teach. I like this new diversity in class, because it totally changes the dynamics of the classroom and the range, making it much more exciting and challenging. (I routinely encourage my female students to purchase a copy of Kathy Jackson's book *The Cornered Cat: A Woman's Guide to Concealed Carry*.)

It's sad that people grow up afraid of guns, and have little experience with the shooting sports. But these new shooters bring a clean slate and a good attitude with them, and seldom have to be untrained of all their bad habits before we train them over again with good ones. These days we are literally taking them step by step from neophyte to advanced concealed carry. You wouldn't believe how many people honestly don't know the difference between a revolver, semi-auto and full automatic. They come to me knowing nothing about how a gun works; how a bullet works; how to hold the gun, or how to use the sights. And it's really fun to start them on their journey into personal defense and the shooting sports.

But then there are a few who come to me as neophytes, and after ten hours of training walk away with a certificate in hand, a concealed pistol license in their pocket, thinking they're ten feet tall and bullet proof. This is a mindset that causes me concern. Fortunately, the vast majority of my students are not like this.

Massad Ayoob once told me that a gun is not a magic talisman whose mere presence will ward away evil. It's just a tool, just a piece of plastic metal and wood, and the tool is only as valuable as your training and proficiency. A long-time friend of mine, Ted Nugent, said "You can run out and buy a guitar, but that doesn't make you a rock star." That's true, and, if anyone should know about that it would be Ted. Firearms work the same way. You can run out and buy a pistol, but that doesn't make you Wyatt Erp. One of my favorite trainers is Rob Pincus from ICE training. Rob stresses that many people believe they will rise to the occasion at the moment of truth. They believe that when that thug steps out from behind the bush and points a gun at you, you'll suddenly become proficient, cool, calm and collected and you'll professionally dispatch the bad guy with ease. This is seldom true. Most people, when under extreme duress, don't rise to the level of their training; they sink to a lower level of proficiency.

> It is highly unlikely that you'll rise to the occasion while faced with deadly force.

Case in point: I can practice all summer shooting my bow and arrow into a bale of straw, but then get out in my tree stand on opening day and miss the first buck that steps in front of me. People perform much better on the range than they do in a life-threatening altercation. So choose the ability and proficiency you want, and then train well beyond that level.

And if you still think you can't be killed, then take a look at the life of Chris Kyle. He was America's deadliest sniper, with more training and combat experience than any of us, yet … he was murdered by a mentally ill person with far lesser skills and experience. And Chris didn't trust this man, so he was already on his guard. Anyone can kill, and anyone can be killed. The sad truth is this: the most skilled gunfighter in the world can be taken down on any given day. He can do everything right and still die. Call it bad luck; call it Karma, call it whatever you like, but, in the end, you're still dead.

> Train for the inevitable ambush. Expect the unexpected and prepare. Live it and breathe it.

There's a great training course out there by Rob Pincus called *Counter Ambush*. The premise of this course is that you will be attacked when you least expect it, perhaps when you are least able to defend yourself. You have to train for the unexpected as well as the expected scenarios.

I highly recommend you eat, drink and live training. Get as much of it as you can, and don't take all your training from one person. Mix it up. Go to the class with an open mind thinking, okay, I'll listen to what he has to say, and, if it works for me and makes sense, then I'll incorporate it into my bag of personal defense tools.

It's easy to come up with excuses not to train. I do it too.

1.   I don't have time.

2.   I don't have the money.

3.   I don't have the right equipment.

4.   I don't want to shoot in front of people.

But all these excuses are surmountable.

1) You can make time for the most important things in your life. We all have twenty-four hours a day and seven days a week. It's just a matter of raising the priority level for your training. I make it a priority in my life to attend (as a student) at least one training school per year. This makes all the difference.

> There is no excuse for not training. All problems are surmountable.

2) You don't have the money? Neither do I. But one class per year is something you can save up for. Tell your friends and family you want cash instead of presents for things like birthdays and Christmas. Where there's a will, there's a way.

3) I can't afford the equipment. I don't have the best equipment in the world either, but you'll find that people in the shooting sports are very generous. One of my former students gave me an Eotech holographic sight. On other occasions I've borrowed equipment for a given class. Pick a training partner or several. You can share motel rooms and gas expenses.

4) I don't want to shoot in front of people. If you can't shoot on the firing line in front of other people, then how do you expect to make good hits under the stress of real combat? If this is you, then shooting in front of an audience is exactly what you need. Force yourself to do it. Tell people about your phobia, and good people will help you train through it into a whole new world of confidence.

One of the problems I have to surmount in my own life is my rigorous training schedule. It seems like whenever I'm on the range, I'm teaching someone else how to shoot or to protect their own family. I've learned to budget in time for my own personal shooting either before or after students arrive at the club. Let's face it, few people will respect or choose a firearms trainer who is a lousy shot. Practice what you preach, and take the extra time to train, train, train! Every chance you get be on the range shooting. If you have no bullets, then dry fire. One great training tool is YouTube. There are loads of great training videos there just for the viewing. But take everything you see on the internet with a grain of salt. Don't incorporate something into your self defense system unless it works for you in your specific situation.

Dave Spaulding from Handgun Combatives has some good training videos which are free for the streaming.

Rob Pincus has an online subscription service for only $34.95 per year where you can watch a myriad of top-notch videos for pennies per viewing.

Check it out at www.personaldefensenetwork.com.

Things to Remember

1. You may be attacked when you least expect it. That's what an "ambush" is.

2. Even the clumsiest of crooks can kill you on any given day, under the right circumstances.

3. Choose the ability and proficiency you want, and then train well beyond that level.

4. The gun is not a magic talisman that wards away evil. It's just a tool. Master the tool, and you'll enhance your chances of prevailing in a gunfight.

Helpful Resources

Here are some very good trainers whom I highly recommend:

Rob Pincus, ICE Training Inc.
www.icetraining.us

Massad Ayoob, Massad Ayoob Group
www.massadayoob.com

Dave Spaulding, Handgun Combatives, Inc
www.handguncombatives.com

Kathy Jackson, Author of *The Cornered Cat: A Woman's Guide to concealed Carry,* www.corneredcat.com

Bob Houzenga & Andy Kemp, Midwest Training Group
www.midwesttraininggroup.net

Matt Canovi, The R.E.A.L Defensive Shooting System
www.mattcanovi.com

Counter Ambush from Rob Pincus is a thorough exploration of both WHY and HOW you should structure your personal defense training to deal with a worst-case scenario ambush situation. *Counter Ambush* is thoroughly supported by over twenty years of research and training in the area of training for all levels of personal defense: Military, Law Enforcement, Security or the Responsible Individual.

Sections include:

-Understanding the need for Counter Ambush Training

-Neuroscience of Counter Ambush Training

-Physiology of Counter Ambush Training

-The Physics of Intuitive Defensive Shooting

-Developing your Counter Ambush Training Program

Combat Focus Shooting: The Science of Intuitive Shooting Skill Development is the cutting edge of understanding how to quickly gain lifesaving firearms skills regardless of your experience, background or the context of your firearms use. Based on working well with what your body does naturally during a dynamic critical incident and focusing on the concept of the balance of speed and precision, this program doesn't just tell you what to do; it explains *why*. This is not just another tool for your toolbox; *Combat Focus® Shooting is the best information the author and his team of instructors have to offer.*

Chapter 5

In this chapter you will learn the following:

- When to fight and when to run.
- All about the warrior mindset.

5

Never Give Up!

ON OCTOBER 19TH, 1950, OVER 120,000 screaming Chinese troops poured across the Yaloo River into North Korea. They attacked the 40,000 United Nations troops on all sides. Most of the UN troops were able to retreat south, but elements of the United States Marine Corps were trapped in the frozen Chosin Reservoir. For several weeks, the frostbitten and beleaguered Marines stood their ground, covering the retreat of the other UN forces, until they were ordered by General MacArthur to fight their way out.

It was during this battle, at an airstrip in Koto-ri, that the commanding officer of the 7th Marines, Lewis (Chesty) Puller was reputed to have summed up the situation like this:

"They're on our right; they're on our left;
they're in front of us; they're behind us.
They can't get away now!"

I like that optimism. I can live with that. By the time it was all over, the Chinese had retaken North Korea, but it was at a tremendous price. In military terminology, the battle was classified as a "pyrrhic" victory for the Chinese.

> Disengage when you can, but sometimes you have to fight!

The word "pyrrhic" originated from the Battle of Asculum in 279BC and in simple terms simply means, "We won the battle, but most of us are dead." Thanks to the valiant stand of the 1st Marine Division at Chosin, the victory for the Chinese was won at too high a cost, and they were forced to halt their advance. After the smoke cleared, 27,500 soldiers lay dead: 25,000 of them were Chinese.

What does this have to do with concealed carry holders? I spent six years in the Marine Corps, and that was enough to change me forever. Thank God they only had to change me once.

"Once a Marine, always a Marine!"
— Master Sergeant Paul Woyshner —

I have always taught that a firearm is a tool of last resort, and I still hold to that. When you can safely disengage; when you can get away from harm without hurting anyone; when you can run away and live to fight another day, then you should do so. It's the wisest course of action. But sometimes that can't be done. The escape routes are blocked. My small children are with me, and to run would be to leave them behind. In cases like these you have no choice but to stand your ground and fight.

When I'm forced to fight, I don't retreat. I don't give up. I counterattack! The best defense is a good offense. I recall in the Marine Corps they made us scream as loud as we could while we attacked "Kill! Kill! Kill!" That did something to me psychologically. It emboldened me and helped me overcome my fear. I imagine it also does something to the person you're attacking as well. I guess I'm suffering from "Jarhead Syndrome": a terminal disease that leaves its victims stubborn, indomitable, and unyielding. When it comes to innocent civilians protecting themselves against bad guys, I wish we could all suffer from Jarhead Syndrome, at least until the fight is over and our loved ones are safe.

> "Jarhead Syndrome": a terminal disease that leaves its victims stubborn, indomitable, and unyielding.

Years ago Florida passed the nation's first "Stand Your Ground" legislation. In simple terms, this means that we don't have to run from the bad guys anymore. We can stand our ground and fight to protect ourselves and our families. What kind of twisted, warped society mandates that its citizens must run from rapists, murderers, and thieves (i.e., the wretched refuse of the Earth) or face possible criminal and civil prosecution? Now I'm just a greasy, old, redneck, bowhunting, Marine, but that just "don't make no sense to me."

And I suspect that a lot of people are feeling the same way, because the "Stand Your Ground" legislation is sweeping the nation like a cleansing wave, washing away fear, and infusing Americans with courage and the will to fight back against rampant crime. Just as concealed carry shall-issue laws have taken over the country, so shall "Stand Your Ground." Most people don't want to be quivering cowards; that's not freedom! That's bondage! It's time for the criminals to fear and flee.

> **Shooting to stop the threat can be a very messy ordeal.**

But the main point I want to get across in this chapter is this: "Once you decide to fight, you must do anything you can to win." Never give up, never give in, fight until the bad guy retreats or drops to the ground.

In my concealed carry classes, people don't want me to say "Shoot to kill!" That's partially a political concern, and has nothing to do with tactics. But it's also about a mindset. When you shoot to stop the threat, rather than shoot to kill, it enables good people to perform an unnatural act and to survive it afterward.

Instead, we say: "Shoot to stop the threat." No matter what you call it, if you accurately rapid fire the center of exposed mass you are likely to stop the threat. Bottom line is this: One way to stop the deadly threat is by causing massive tissue damage and blood loss to our attacker. If they turn and run, great! It saves us all the price of expensive premium self defense ammo. If they choose to stand and fight, well, I can live with that too. But once I decide to fight, my attitude has to be that of a United States Marine: "I will never lose. I will never retreat. I will win!"

I love the Marine Corps. They make me feel safe. And I especially love the way they speak their mind, despite the rash of political correctness infecting our nation. Because I am a Marine, I understand the way we think. But most people don't have that luxury.

> *"There are only two kinds of people who understand Marines: Marines and those who have met them in battle. Everyone else has a second-hand opinion."*

Unknown —

> ## Make your attacker know you firsthand. Think like a Marine. Fight like a Marine.

Make your attacker know you first-hand. Think like a Marine. Fight like a Marine. Never give up. Fight until one of you drops. Your family and all of society are depending on you.

The other day I was in a mood for a goofy movie, so I popped in *Monty Python and the Holy Grail*. In the best comedy, there is always an element of truth. I was impressed by the Black Knight, who stood his ground and fought against King Arthur. A summary of the battle ensues below:

The brave and noble King Arthur comes to a bridge, which is defended by the Black Knight. He asks the Black Knight to join his court at Camelot and to help in his quest for the Holy Grail. The Black Knight turns him down, so King Arthur begins to move by on his way across the bridge. The Black Knight finally speaks.

"None shall pass!"

"What?"

"None shall pass!"

King Arthur tries to reason with him.

"I have no quarrel with you good Sir Knight, but I must

cross this bridge."

"Then you shall die!"

King Arthur is surprised but quickly turns indignant.

"I command you as King of the Britons to stand aside!"

The Black Knight stands his ground.

"I move for no man!"

Resolved to cross the bridge, King Arthur and the Black Knight become locked in deadly sword-to-sword combat. But the king gains the advantage by cutting off the Black Knight's left arm. Blood gushes out for a moment, but quickly subsides. The king assumes victory, but the Black Knight refuses to yield.

> Once you decide to fight, you bite, kick, scratch and scream.

"Tis but a scratch!"

"A scratch? Your arms off!"

"No it isn't!"

"Well, what's that then?"

"I've had worse."

"You lie."

"Come on you pansy!"

They continue to fight until the king hacks off the knight's other arm. The king assumes victory again, but the knight begins kicking him for all he's worth. King Arthur tries to convince him to stop, but the knight refuses to give up.

"It's just a flesh wound," he says.

The king is forced to cut off the Black Knight's right leg. The knight, undeterred, continues to hop on one leg and come at the king with head butts.

"Come here!"

"What are you going to do? Bleed on me?"

The knight replies.

"I'm invincible!"

The left leg is hacked off and the Black Knight's torso and head plop onto the ground. The Black Knight looks up and says.

"All right. We'll call it a draw."

The king rides away with his servant as the Black Knight screams after him.

"Oh, I see. Running away? Come back here and take what's coming to you! I'll bite your legs off!"

So I say to all of you, never give up. Your attitude must be that of Major General Oliver P. Smith, USMC, Korea, December 1950.

"Retreat Hell! We're just attacking in another direction!"

It has been said that attitude is 90 percent of everything in life. I think it's closer to 95. I'm not saying to be stupid, like the Black Knight. I'm saying be brave. Bravery is not the absence of fear, it is the presence of courage in the face of danger.

Choose your battles wisely, but once you choose, never give up. There's no future in capitulation. Bite their legs off! Win!

Things to Remember

1. When you can safely disengage, retreat is usually the wisest option.

2. When you cannot disengage, fight with all you've got.

3. Never give up! Never surrender. Live the warrior mindset.

Helpful Resources

These books are available on Amazon.com

The Art of War
written by Sun Tzu

Chosin: Heroic Ordeal of the Korean War
written by Eric Hammel

Marine! The Life of Chesty Puller
written by Burke Davis

Guidebook for Marines
Marine Corps Association

Mark Walters & Kathy Jackson

Whether you are new to the concept of armed defense or have long since made it a part of a prudent lifestyle, you'll find much that is useful in this book. Read it the way Kathy and Mark wrote it, that is, don't just look at it, but study it for its lessons! – Massad Ayoob Founder, Lethal Force Institute Author of *In the Gravest Extreme* –

These are serious words from Massad, the Master of self defense! Don't rely on others to protect yourself and your loved ones. "Lessons from Armed America" is the essential primer for self defense. Kathy and Mark are the experts that answer all your questions on stalking, real-life firefights, prevention and awareness, as well as carjacking and use of nonlethal force. They tell it like it is with candor and compassion, speaking through both experience and well-thought-out research. If you're serious about protecting your family, this is the one book you MUST read!

PART II

SAFETY

Chapter 6

In this chapter you will learn the following:

- How to safely handle a pistol.
- All about children and guns.
- Who is authorized to handle your gun.

"And the bottom line remains that there is no such thing as an accidental discharge, only negligent discharges. It is never a hardware problem, always a human mistake. Period. So don't make the mistake."

— Ted Nugent —

6

Rules for Gun Handling

HAVE YOU EVER CUSSED AT YOUR computer? I have, many times. The problem with computers, is that they always do precisely what they're "told" to do, regardless of what you "want" them to do. In that regard, firearms are the same way. When I pull the trigger, the gun goes "bang." When I point the gun at a person, then pull the trigger, someone gets hurt or perhaps even dies. It's really quite simple.

But there are a few big differences between computers and guns.

1) Computers don't blow up and kill you if you push the wrong key sequence. I've seen that happen only a few times, and that was always in Hollywood movies.

2) Computers have a key sequence called "control Z" which comes in very handy when you make a mistake. If I ac-

cidently delete some text I need, it's not gone forever. I simply press control z and the missing text comes back like magic.

I've never found a gun with a "control z" option. Once you shoot an innocent person, the damage is done, with no way to bring them back. Rookie cops, and even veteran police officers, sometimes make mistakes by shooting the wrong people. Wouldn't it be great if they could simply press control z and make everything right again? But we can't do that, and I doubt the control z function will ever be available on any firearm.

> Guns are supposed to be dangerous. People are supposed to be safe.

My students sometimes ask me why I choose to carry a firearm without a mechanical safety. The answer is simple. Guns aren't supposed to be safe; to the contrary, guns are extremely dangerous. That's the way they're designed. And if your gun isn't dangerous, then it's defective and you should take it back to the gun store for a refund. Now, if you want a gun with a mechanical safety, go ahead and buy one. But, for me, I don't want another step added to my draw sequence. I want to keep it simple. Don't allow your mechanical safety to give you a false sense of security. Safeties sometimes malfunction. Don't trust them. I have one pistol with a mechanical safety, and half the time I draw it, the safety has somehow become disengaged, either through the normal motions of life, or for some other reason unknown to me.

Guns are dangerous; therefore, people must be safe. Gun safety has and always will be dictated by the gray matter between the gun owner's ears. If you know the rules and follow them to the letter religiously, then your guns become safe in your hands. If you're not safe, then do the world a favor and don't carry a gun until you are. Gun safety is a conscious action that has to be done out of habit every single time you touch a firearm. In that regard it's very simple. If you follow the rules, your gun will never hurt an innocent person.

So that begs the question, "If it's so simple, then why are there still gun accidents?" On page 211 of Ted Nugent's book *God, Guns, and Rock-n-roll* Ted makes this ingeniously basic assertion:

> *"And the bottom line remains that there is no such thing as an accidental discharge, only negligent discharges. It is never a hardware problem, always a human mistake. Period. So don't make the mistake."*

And, of course, Ted is right. After all, he's Ted. And with that in mind, let's go over the rules for gun handling.

> *Note: The following safety rules are my versions of the rules taught to all concealed carry instructors across the nation. They are tried and true, but I have added commentary based on my experience.*

1. The gun must ALWAYS be pointed in a safe direction.

This is the number one rule of gun safety, because "safe direction" is defined as any direction whereas if the gun were to discharge no one would be struck by the bullet.

Most people have enough sense to know you shouldn't point a loaded gun at another person. But some don't. I'm on the gun range training every week, and last year alone I had five people point loaded guns at my chest. This year I had a man point a loaded pistol at my head. He said it was an accident, but I was upset nonetheless. I guess I'm quirky that way.

On the gun range I have seen the most intelligent people do the most stupid things. People like to make disparaging remarks about rednecks. The most well known is this: "Hey Bubba, hold on to my beer. Watch this!"

But I've had doctors, lawyers and school teachers make mistakes with firearms for a variety of reasons. But, in the end, all these mistakes are unnecessary. Do not become cocky with a gun. Do not become desensitized to the danger of the gun. Guns are inanimate objects; they are tools which function in accordance with their wielders. When you follow the rules, you are safe. When you break the rules, innocent people you love can die.

> When intelligent people get nervous, they do stupid things.

2.   Your finger must not touch the trigger until you're on target ready to shoot.

This is the rule I see violated most often on the range. Most people know better than to point a gun at someone, but, for some people, their finger automatically moves to the trigger every time they pick up a firearm. It's like it's in their DNA and they just can't help it.

Sadly enough, by the time some students get to my class, they've been shooting guns for decades and have already developed bad habits. Everything we do out of habit is really nothing more than muscle memory, something we do without thinking. I tell my class there are only two ways to flunk:

1) If you exhibit a pattern of poor safety habits on the range, you will not receive a certificate from me today.

2) If you're the kind of person who tends to hear voices other people can't, then, at least for today, don't answer the voices.

I've flunked a few people in my day, and one lady in particular comes to mind. She tried desperately all afternoon to keep her finger off the trigger, but she just couldn't do it. I told her to go home and come back in a week. In the meantime, she was to buy a toy gun at the dollar store. I had her walk around her house all week with the gun in her pocket. Every few minutes she consciously drew her toy gun with her trigger finger down the slide. In accordance with the rules of muscle memory, it took her thousands of repetitions to keep her finger off the trigger until ready to shoot. But, a week later she came back and proudly received her concealed carry certificate.

NOTE

When you clench your fist, all fingers and thumb naturally come together. It is unnatural to wrap your three fingers around the pistol grip while keeping your index finger straight along the frame or slide. However, when gripping your gun, this is exactly what you must do to keep your finger off the trigger. After thousands of repetitions, it will become second nature.

3. The gun must be kept unloaded until you're ready to use it.

> An unloaded gun is just a very expensive club.

Every once in a while, a concealed carry holder will tell me they carry a gun, but the chamber is empty or they have the gun in their holster and the magazine is in their left pocket. They do this for the noble and well-intentioned reason of increased safety. But here's the problem: they don't understand the anatomy of a gun fight. Most personal attacks are extremely sudden and extremely violent.

If you're expecting the gun to save your life, then it needs to be loaded. After all, an unloaded gun is just a very expensive club, and not a very good club at that. According to FBI crime statistics, the average fire fight lasts only three seconds. Think about it. Do you really want to spend the first two or three seconds of a three-second gun fight trying to load your firearm?

Now, of course, if the gun is not being used for personal defense, then it should be stored unloaded. When you're transporting the gun it should be unloaded, locked in a case and separate from the ammunition. But when the gun is safely in your holster and you expect it to save your life, the gun must be loaded.

NOTE

It is important to note that firearm transport laws vary from state to state. Take the time to learn the transport laws of your jurisdiction.)

> Things look different in the dark than in the light of day.

And remember the age-old adage, "All guns are always loaded." If you treat every gun as if it were loaded, even when it's not, you can't go wrong. It's amazing how many people thought the gun was unloaded ... right up until they heard the blast.

4. Always be certain of your target and where your bullets will impact.

This is especially important when you're carrying concealed out and about in public. Whether you're at Walmart or a gas station or the grocery store, you're going to be with other people. And it is your responsibility to keep these people safe from any bullet leaving your gun.

First, let's talk about low-light conditions. As I've already said, most altercations occur at night with limited visibility. Bad guys like the cover of darkness, and this makes it tougher for the good guy to take good shots and to know where the bullets are going.

Knowing your target is tough in the dark. Deer hunters face this problem all the time. The deer come in just about sunrise and then again at sundown. As a deer hunter myself, I understand the feeling of wanting the shadowed form we see in the pre-dawn light to be a deer. I want it to be a deer. I want it to have antlers – big ones! But patience is a virtue, and you should hold off until you can positively identify your target. Again, remember control z? You don't have one on your gun.

> People are going to live or die based on decisions you make.

Knowing what's beyond your target is just as important, especially in a populated area. You're safely behind cover in the convenience store, the clerk can't get the register open and the bad guy is about to shoot. It doesn't help matters if you shoot and miss the bad guy but hit the twenty-three-year-old single mom behind the counter. Take the time to move and get her out of the line of fire.

It's also important to know what is between you and your target. Are there children running around in front of you? Is there steel, cement or wood in front of you which can cause a deadly ricochet?

Take these things into consideration before making your

shot. Remember, people are going to live or die based on decisions you make. So make good decisions.

5.   Know how to operate your gun in all conditions.

About half the people coming to my classes these days are new to pistol shooting. As such, they don't yet own their concealed carry gun. The typical way they handle this problem is by borrowing a gun from a friend or relative or by renting a firearm from me. In both scenarios, they have little idea how to operate that firearm. This is a potentially dangerous situation.

> Become an expert at "running your gun."

In the past I've seen people struggling with the slide, trying to pull it back but with little success. In their haste and determination to open the slide, they don't realize that the mechanical safety latch has to be disengaged before the slide will move. In the meantime, they're struggling so hard with the gun, that they don't realize they're pointing it at themselves or the person next to them.

The skill set necessary to operate your gun is called "running your gun." Every gun is different. Some pistols have lots of bells and whistles like mechanical safety latches, slide locks, magazine release buttons and take-down levers. You have to know how all these operate, and you must have the strength and coordination to make these movements. And since most altercations occur in low-light conditions, you have to be able to do it without looking at the gun.

I'm reminded of the movie *Major Payne* with Damon Wayans who plays the part of a seasoned combat Marine. In one scene he is blindfolded, hanging from a bar upside down by his feet. He is field stripping his pistol, cleaning it and reassembling it. We don't do that in my concealed carry class for obvious reasons, but if everyone could, there would be fewer safety violations because everyone would know how to use their gun safely.

6.   Never try to catch a falling gun.

If you handle a firearm long enough, it's not unreasonable to assume you might drop it. After all, we drop our car keys, pencils, books, cell phones, all types of objects every single day. But here's the difference: cell phones don't have triggers, bullets and barrels. Your car keys will never shoot you in the head as you reach down to grab them on the way down. This is difficult advice to take because it's just a natural reflex action to try and catch something as it falls. We do it all the time. But you must force yourself to let the gun fall. I don't care if it's an expensive match-grade gun with engraved slide and pearl grips. You let it hit the ground – even if it's pavement or cement.

> **Always keep your gun properly oiled and cleaned.**

After that, don't just pick it up and fire away. First, safely unload the gun and field strip it to check for any damage. If you find any cracks or things that just don't look right, take it to a licensed gunsmith for repair. Never fire a gun unless you know it's in good working order.

Of course, the best solution for all this is to never drop your gun. While this makes sense, it's not an iron-clad guarantee. While you can lessen the chances of your own clumsiness through proper gun handling and good muscle memory, you can never totally eliminate the possibility. Just be careful and learn how to properly draw your gun with a good, firm grip.

7. Keep your gun safely maintained.

This isn't rocket science. Every time you shoot your gun, it needs to be cleaned. It's like taking out the trash; the longer you put it off the worse it's going to be. Dirt, grime and powder residue will build up over time and cause your gun to malfunction in a myriad of ways. By keeping the gun clean, you lessen the chances of these malfunctions occurring.

The gun should also be properly protected from moisture. If you get caught in a rainstorm, even though you haven't fired it, you should clean the pistol and put on a coat of oil.

> 9 millimeter and 40 caliber ammo do not work and play well together.

A light coat for a gun you carry every day, and a heavier coat for one you'll put in storage. Usually a liquid gun conditioner will suffice. Everyone has their favorites, and the vast majority of them do a great job.

When you clean your gun, you should always check it for stress cracks or fractures of any kind. If you find anything that just doesn't look right, do not shoot it until it's been checked out by a licensed, competent gunsmith.

8. Use the right ammunition.

The biggest problem we have with this is mixing up 9 millimeter ammo with .40 caliber. Let's face it, they look a lot alike. The 9 millimeter cartridge is just 1 millimeter smaller in diameter than a .40 caliber round, so it's easy to confuse them. I have to admit that I've made this mistake myself. I own both .40 caliber and 9 millimeter pistols, and sometimes I shoot them both on the range on the same outing. Keep them separated out on the range, 9 millimeter on one end of the staging table and .40 caliber on the other.

What happens when you load 9 millimeter into a .40 caliber handgun? Well, nothing … until you press the trigger. The round usually goes off, but it won't eject properly. When you manually extract the empty brass casing you'll see that the casing is barrelled out for most of its length. Bear in mind that the chamber of the gun is designed to tightly press up against the brass casing, thus, containing the explosion upon firing. Brass is a soft metal, so it gives way to the explosion and flares out. If the chamber is unable to contain the explosion, then the gun may come apart in your hand. So be very careful not to mix your ammo.

Another potential problem is shooting high-pressure ammo through a pistol which is not rated for the higher chamber pressures, This is usually labeled as +p or +p+ ammunition. It is typically used in personal defense ammo as it contains a higher powder load resulting in higher chamber pressures, increased velocity and kinetic energy. Most people will use high pressure ammo in their carry guns for marginal calibers like 9 millimeter, .38 special and smaller. The higher pressures give it just a little more stopping power in the form of increased penetration. I carry +p ammo in my 9 millimeter carry gun, and recommend that you do as well, provided you can handle the slight increase in recoil.

Every person gets only one set of eyes and ears. So protect them.

Also be careful not to shoot magnum rounds through a non-magnum handgun; this can cause a catastrophic failure (i.e., the gun can blow up in your hands.)

9. Eye and ear protection must always be worn while shooting.

Protect your eyes and ears as God gives only one pair per human and there is no warranty. I've been shooting extensively for fifteen years and have slight hearing loss because I didn't think this rule applied to me. I was wrong. You can use ear plugs or shooting muffs.

Ear plugs come in a variety of types. Some are disposable; others are more elaborate and can be custom fitted to your ears.

Shooting muffs can be mechanical or electronic. Mechanical muffs tend to be less expensive, but require no batteries. Electronic types require batteries and the good ones can cost into the hundreds of dollars. They are helpful while teaching on the range, because they amplify voices, but shut out louder noises like gunfire. I can also use the amplification function while deer hunting to help me hear walking animals from farther away.

Choose the hearing protection that works best for you. During a prolonged shooting session or class I double up on my protection, wearing both plugs and muffs in an attempt to protect what hearing I have left.

Eye protection need not be elaborate and expensive. It can be a pair of sun glasses or plastic lens safety glasses. Just make sure the protective lens completely covers the eye and you'll be fine. Some people have trouble shooting because they're either near-sighted or far-sighted. Just remember that your attention is on the front sight, and it should be clear and in focus. Some of my students have gone to the eye doctor to have special shooting glasses made for them. I have mixed feelings about this. If your purpose in shooting is to prepare for personal defense, then the glasses you practice with on the range should be the same glasses you wear every day.

10. Drugs, alcohol and guns do not mix.

Most people are smart enough to know that guns and drugs and alcohol don't mix. But some aren't, and I wish this minority of people would not own guns, because they make the rest of us look bad (not to mention the damage they do to the innocent people around them.)

With alcohol, the problem arises when people try to judge for themselves how much alcohol is too much. In my opinion, if you're going to be carrying a gun for personal defense, then one drink may be too much. Alcohol dulls your senses, your reflexes and your reaction time. No one ever becomes a better gun fighter after a few drinks. (They might think they're better, faster, stronger, and more good looking … but they're not.) After one drink you may still be legally able to carry your gun, and perhaps even not impaired and physically able to use the gun for personal defense, but usually this is what happens.

1. After the first drink you say to yourself. *I feel fine. My head is clear and I can still focus.* So you have another.

> No one gets smarter when they drink.

2. After the second drink you say to yourself. *I feel even better now than I did after the first drink.* So you go ahead and have a third, a fourth, fifth, etc., until you drive away in your car, get pulled over with a blood alcohol content of .03 or .08 or even higher. In many states this is enough to get your concealed pistol license revoked or

suspended.

If you decide to drink, then take the firearm out of the mix. Take the time and effort to ensure your firearm is secure in accordance with the laws of your jurisdiction. There's a reason cops call alcohol "stupid juice."

> Never carry a gun when your judgement is impaired.

Now let's talk about drug use and guns. During class I'll go around the room and ask students to name off a drug. Most people give answers like this: heroin, meth, LSD, cocaine.

And to be sure these are all very dangerous illegal drugs that should not be mixed with firearms. But many times people focus so much on illegal drugs that they fail to recognize legal drugs as potential safety hazards when coupled with firearms.

Prescription painkillers are an example of this. Many of my students are older, which means they've had back surgery, hip and knee replacements, or arthritis. All of these can cause severe pain requiring strong medication to alleviate the discomfort and enhance mobility. I advise my students on medication to ask their doctor about the possible side effects of the medication. The potential problem here is doctors have lawyers who often advise against taking on any added liability. So when you go to your doctor and say "Hey Doc. Is it okay if I shoot my guns while on this medication?" you may not get a straight answer. However, if you modify your question to be "Hey Doc. Is it okay if I drive a car or operate heavy equipment while on this medication?" Then you're more likely to get a clear, useful answer.

The basic common-sense rule is this: If your senses or judgement are impaired (even a little) then you should not be handling firearms. This could entail something as innocent as an over-the-counter night-time cold medicine with something in it to help you sleep at night. For me, after taking this type of medicine the night before, I'll wake up the next morning feeling drowsy. When this happens I wait a few hours to strap on my firearm, giving me a chance to wake up fully before adding a gun to the mix.

11. Create a list of people authorized to use your guns.

When I ask my class for an example of an unauthorized person, the immediate answer is always children. That's an important example, but it doesn't end there. Here's a list that you can start with and add to as you see fit.

- Kids
- People known to have poor judgement
- Those who cannot legally possess a firearm
- Those with inadequate training

Children and guns - Children should never have free and unrestricted access to firearms. This is just courting disaster. But children must have access to superior firearms training, and it must be given under the supervision of parents or their designee. Good parents know their children better than anyone else, so they are the best judge of when a child is ready to handle firearms.

> **Properly train your children to respect and handle firearms under your supervision.**

I believe firearm safety training for children should start as soon as they are mobile and are capable of understanding the word "no." For toddler and elementary age children, I highly recommend the Eddie Eagle Gun Safety training program created by the National Rifle Association (NRA). This program is simple and easy to understand. Teach your children that when they see an unsupervised firearm, they are to do the following:

STOP

DON'T TOUCH

LEAVE THE AREA

TELL A GROWN UP

Some of my students come to me with a different approach. They prefer to child-proof their home. But here's the problem.

1) There's no such thing as a child-proof home. Babies start out lying on a blanket and then they crawl. So you move the breakable items up out of reach. Then they learn to pull themselves up and walk around the coffee table, so you move the forbidden items higher. But once they learn to climb it's Katy bar the door. Small children can climb book shelves, cupboards, desks, anything with or without a handle.

> The parent should know when a child is ready for firearms.

2) Even if you could child-proof your home, what happens when you visit other homes? You have no guarantee that other families will be as conscientious as yourself about locking up their guns and making their homes safe.

I believe it's best to train your child to obey your rules and restrictions and to always keep your guns locked up and inaccessible to them. By doing this you're teaching them at a young age that there are boundaries and rules, and that they can't just do anything they want at the moment. Respect for authority and the rule of law is something they can take into their teen years and adulthood, thereby enhancing their chances at survival and success in life.

Another question I frequently get is this: *At what age should I start teaching my child how to shoot?* I start that job at around four years old, but it's done under very strict circumstances. At that young age they can't possibly fire a gun safely by themselves so I help them. I hold the gun and I allow them to place their hands around my hands while I'm shooting. They are between my arms and behind the muzzle, so it's totally safe. But it allows them to experience the shooting sports in a safe manner at a young age. And these days, with video games, television and social networking, you have to catch kids early if you're going to interest them in anything without a computer screen.

When do you allow them to shoot unsupervised? Now that's a tougher question and it's not black and white. Every child is different, so the answer is always best decided on a case-case basis. You know your child, but you should always err on the side of safety.

> Don't take chances with the lives of your children.

When my son was ten years old I bought him a BB gun. I didn't quite trust him, so I never let him shoot it unless I was there with him. I painstakingly taught him the rules of safety and all about marksmanship. He'd been shooting frequently for six months when he came to me and said he wanted to shoot. It was the end of a very hard day, and I was relaxing in my recliner, totally exhausted. I did not want to get up out of that chair, so I asked him what the safety rules are. He repeated them back to me verbatim. Satisfied that I'd taught him well, I eased back into my chair and told him to go have fun but to stay safe.

Five minutes later I heard a very loud "crack!" I remember thinking, *That doesn't sound like a BB gun.* I got up from my chair and walked over to the sliding glass door leading to the deck. It was a double-paned glass door which was now a single-paned door. I looked down and saw shattered glass all over, so I opened the door and stepped out. There, in the center of the deck, was an unscathed Mountain Dew can. I looked over and saw my son walking up, dragging his BB gun behind him. I said, "Son, is that the can you were shooting at?" He sheepishly nodded his head. "Well, why did you put it in front of the glass window?" His answer was both profound and obvious, "Because I could see it better up there."

> **People with bad judgment should not handle firearms.**

My first thought was *Wow! That's really stupid.* My second thought was *I'm glad I didn't buy him a shotgun.* In reality, he was a very intelligent person, but what he lacked was perspective and experience. Here's the thing with children: they're so young that they've never had anything really bad happen to them yet. Bad things, tragedies, painful things in our lives; those are the experiences that teach us wisdom, and my son hadn't learned that yet. Cause and effect is something that is taught slowly, through time and usually has a pain penalty attached to it.

Here's the bottom line: don't trust your children unsupervised with guns. They need your wisdom, your experience and your understanding of cause and effect. Get off your lazy butt and shoot with them. It's a bonding experience that will last a lifetime and give them a good start in life.

People known to have poor judgement - I come from a redneck family. There! I admit it! Nothing wrong with that so long as you have good character and you follow the law. I have lots of brothers and sisters, and, over the years, we've married, divorced, remarried, had lots of children, who have, in turn, had lots of children. Let's just say the Coryell get-togethers are large and full of personality.

All of us know at least one person with poor judgement. It may be a friend or a relative, but when they ask to borrow our car, deep down inside, we wince, knowing that it may not come back to us in one piece.

DO NOT let these people touch your guns! They are future Darwin award recipients, and you don't want to contribute to their demise or cause pain and suffering to other innocent people. You are potentially civilly and criminally liable for every bullet that leaves your gun, even if you're not the one firing it.

Those who cannot legally possess a firearm - The United States government has a list of people who are not allowed to possess a firearm, and some states expand on that list, so learn the legalities of your jurisdiction before loaning out your firearms. The federal list goes like this: (At the time of this writing)

- convicted felons
- illegal drug users
- people committed to a mental institution
- People who are not US citizens or legal residents
- People who have renounced their US citizenship
- Those convicted of a misdemeanor crime of do-

mestic violence

Caution:

The above list is not considered to be all-inclusive, and some jurisdictions have laws more restrictive than federal law, so always consult a competent legal professional licensed to practice in your jurisdiction before loaning your guns to anyone questionable.

Those with inadequate training - This is just common sense, but since common sense isn't as common as it used to be, it warrants clarification. Just because someone tells you they know how to handle guns, that doesn't mean they're safe with guns. When screening someone for a basic concealed carry class, I have to ascertain they are safe and responsible and have adequate knowledge of the safety rules. Some of the things people tell me are really quite comical. For example: "Oh, yeah. Sure. I've been around guns my whole life!"

> **Get quality training before handling firearms.**

I have to ask myself What does that really mean?

Were they raised in an apartment over a gun store?

Are they a drug dealer?

Most of the time it means, "I have no formal training in firearms, especially pistols, but my dad owned one and I went deer hunting, so that means I'm an expert, and I don't have to go to your beginner's class."

Adequate training should not be overlooked or minimized. Don't let anyone have access to your firearms unless they know the basic safety rules and have adequate, formal training in marksmanship and gun handling. These self-professed experts are usually the ones who show up in the local newspaper saying "I didn't know the gun was loaded." Flee from the self-taught pistol expert. They cannot be trusted.

In conclusion - There should be a small list of people who have access to your firearms. If the list is too small, then you could die. Case in point, three men break into your home, catch you unaware, and proceed to beat you to a bloody pulp. Your wife is sitting on the sofa knitting. She calmly looks up and says, "Sorry honey, I would be happy to help you, but I don't know the combination to the gun safe."

Get your spouse and all other responsible members of your household adequate training in firearms and personal defense. Move them from the liability column into the asset column; they are potential allies.

On the other hand, if your list of authorized people is too large then you could also die. Be very careful when you make your list. Personal feelings should not be a factor. Yes, I know someone could be offended if you deny them access, because you'll have to tell them why. That's a relationship problem though, and outside the scope of this book. Better to have a friend upset for a time than to have an innocent person hurt or killed.

12. All guns are always loaded.

This rule was popularized by Colonel Jeff Cooper, founder of Gunsite firearms training academy. It seems like many of these negligent discharges (which kill people) occur when someone thinks the gun isn't loaded when it really is.

> The gun is always loaded - even when you know it's empty.

Be careful not to desensitize yourself to the deadly nature of firearms. I talk to many people who work in gun stores and it drives them crazy when people point guns all over the place. By necessity they have customers point guns at them on a daily basis. If they correct the customer, then he becomes offended and goes to another store.

That's why I use training guns in my classes. They are just blue pieces of molded plastic (firearm facsimiles) that can be used safely for training purposes without the possibility of desensitizing people. You should always feel uncomfortable when someone points a gun at you - even when you know it's unloaded. By extension, you should also feel uncomfortable when you point a loaded gun at another human. If you are pointing a gun at another human, it's because you are going to kill him. That can be summed up in Colonel Cooper's second firearm safety rule. "Never let the muzzle cover anything you are not willing to destroy."

Things to Remember

1. Treat all guns as if they are loaded.

2. Never point a gun at another person unless you want to kill them.

3. Do not give access of your guns to untrustworthy people.

4. Never allow children to shoot guns without competent supervision.

5. Always keep your guns locked up.

Helpful Resources

These books are available on Amazon.com

A Family Guide to Gun Safety
written by Chris Ford

God, Guns and Rock-n-Roll
written by Ted Nugent

Personal Protection in the Home
published by the National Rifle Association

Concealed Carry and Home Defense Fundamentals
written by Michael Martin
Published by United States Concealed Carry Association

Just the Basics: A Guide for the New Shooter
written by Bill Keller

Here I am with Lieutenant General Jerry Boykin (retired) at
Cornerstone University. The general is a founding member
of Delta Force and later became the commanding general
of the Special Operations Command. Presently he is the
Executive Vice President of the Family Research Council. I
was honored to be on the general's personal security detail
several times as he toured, speaking about the dangers of
Islamic terrorism. I learned very quickly that he enjoyed
teasing Marines. That's okay, because I was quick to tease
him back. He's a very good man.

This picture was taken in Chicago, Illinois at a class taught by Massad Ayoob called "*Judicious Use of Deadly Force*". It was 20 hours of intensive training on the legal and emotional ramifications of being involved in a lethal shoot-out. The Massad Ayoob Group gives some of the best training in the world. You should make time to train with Massad. Massad is the master. (Go to www.ayoob.com for info on his classes.) Two friends and MAG Instructors, Bob Houzenga and Andy Kemp, are kneeling in the front row.

Massad is kneeling in the number one spot and I am standing behind him. Andy and Bob are kneeling in the number 4 and 5 positions, respectively.

(Photo courtesy of Vernon Jenewein)

Midwest Tactical teaches all across Michigan, but our home range is here in Hastings at the Barry County Conservation Club. We also teach in Hamilton Rod & Gun Club, Fennville Rod & Gun Club, and Caledonia Sportsman's Club.

(Photo courtesy of Jared Fulton)

After two days of Combat Focus Shooting class, we posed for the camera with Instructor Rob Pincus. I enjoy Rob's training. What he teaches makes sense to me, and I try to pass it on to my own students whenever possible.

Here I am with Kathy Jackson, firearms instructor and author of "The Cornered Cat: A Women's Guide to Concealed Carry." I am proud to serve as Kathy's publisher. Her book has been our #1 best seller for 5 years running. Kathy is a great ambassador to the cause, bringing in and training women shooters all over the country.

As an author, publisher, and USCCA firearms instructor, I get to spend time with some great people in the firearms industry. Here are Tim Schmidt, founder of the United States Concealed Carry Association, and Mark Walters, host of Armed American Radio. Both are friends and men of great character. Tim is the slightly taller gentleman on the right. The guy's a beanstalk!

Here I am with two of my funniest Second Amendment friends.
Kenn Blanchard on the left is also one of my authors who wrote
"Black Man with a Gun: Reloaded." Rick Ector on my right is
a fellow concealed carry instructor teaching in Detroit at Rick's
Firearms Academy.

In the past 30 years I've introduced all my children to firearms. I enjoy teaching them to be safe and how to protect themselves and their family.

Nathan Nephew is on the left and Brian Jeffs is on the right of me. Brian and Nate are co-founders of Michigan Open Carry as well as co-authors of the book *My Parents Open Carry*. I serve with them on the Board of Directors for the group I founded called The Second Amendment March. Guys like this make it fun to fight for the right to keep and bear arms.

Here I am with my friend and fellow instructor Joel Fulton as we review his comments on my manuscript. The two of us have been training civilians and fighting for the right to keep and bear arms for many years. Joel co-owns Freedom Firearms in Battle Creek, Michigan with his brother Jared. It's an excellent gun store and indoor range. If you are ever in the area, be sure to stop in and say hello.

Chapter 7

In this chapter you will learn the following:

- The different types of handguns available.
- All about revolvers vs semi-automatics.
- The strengths and weaknesses of various handguns.

7

Choosing the Gun

MY STUDENTS ALWAYS ASK ME "Should I buy a revolver or a semi-automatic pistol for my carry gun?" And I always answer with brevity. "Yes."

Selecting your concealed carry gun isn't that simple. There is no "one" magic super gun that is best for all people. It's a highly personal decision that should never be based on only one criteria, and is almost always a compromise.

I can't tell you how many times I've had people come to class with a brand new gun, still in the plastic, and, as we stand on the firing line, they appear frustrated because they can't consistently hit the target. I watch them for a while, and finally, they ask me, "What can I do to fix this?" My answer to them is never received with joy and elation. I tell them "Buy a different gun, one that fits you and that you can comfortably shoot. Someone who just spent $700 on a gun doesn't want to hear that, so I quickly follow up with rational support for my statement. (The last thing I want is for them to "shoot the messenger.")

There are a lot of factors to consider before buying your first handgun for concealed carry. I'm going to go over them now, so that you can make the best decision possible.

Caliber

The majority of self-defense instructors recommend a minimum of .38 special, 9 millimeter or larger to have sufficient stopping power for use in personal defense. While I agree with that in a general way, I understand that sometimes people just can't handle the medium to larger calibers.

I was teaching a class once, and I was on the firing line with an 82-year-old lady. She was shooting a .22 caliber pistol. She had a good group, and was well on her way to becoming a proficient shooter. Beside us on the firing line was a very large and powerful man. He stood about six and a half feet tall and was 250 pounds of muscle. He was shooting a .45 caliber semi-auto. The little, old lady would go "pop, pop" when she fired, and the big body builder would go "BOOM! BOOM!"

> Shoot the highest caliber that you can safely and accurately control.

I noticed that everytime the lady shot her .22 caliber, the big man beside us would start to laugh. After a while it got on my nerves and I yelled cease fire.

"What are you laughing at?" I said.

He replied, "What is she going to do with that thing, piss somebody off?"

I thought for a few seconds and asked the lady for her pistol. She carefully handed it to me, because it was loaded. I held it in my hand, with finger off the trigger and the muzzle pointed down range and told him, "I'd like you to hold your hand out in front of me." The big man hesitated before asking, "Why? What are you going to do?"

I responded confidently, "Well, I'm going to shoot you five times in the hand."

His response was a quick, reflex action. "What! Are you nuts!"

I said, "What's the big deal? It's just a twenty-two."

Now, obviously, I wasn't going to shoot him or put him in harm's way in any manner. I just wanted to make a point. "No sane person wants to be shot with a gun of any caliber."

> The 1st rule to a gunfight is "Bring a gun!"

Do I carry a .22 caliber? No, I don't. But that's because I can handle a larger caliber. The general rule is this: "Shoot the largest caliber that you can safely and effectively control." And that brings us to our next point.

Recoil

I was once teaching a private lesson to a woman. She was shooting a brand, new Smith and Wesson J-frame revolver with a Titanium alloy frame. It's a beautiful gun and quite popular for concealed carry for those who like simplicity, compactness and light weight. But she was getting quite frustrated because she couldn't hit the paper target. Usually I can watch someone shoot for several minutes, analyze their results, then make some changes to get them on target. But this woman had no bullet grouping. She told me that it was a new gun and that it hadn't been sighted in yet. I explained to her that the sights on this particular revolver were fixed and can't be adjusted. She didn't believe me and insisted that I shoot her gun. I did. I shot five times into the paper and produced a one-inch group.

> The lighter the recoil, the faster you can make accurate shots.

She looked at me like I was super human. "How did you do that?" As I am prone to do, I answered her question with a question of my own. "Let me ask you something, Does it hurt your hands when the gun goes off?" Her eyes lit up. "Yes, it feels like I just hit an oak tree with a ball bat." I smiled. "Yes, me too. It hurts a lot." The rest of our conversation went like this.

HER: "So how did you hit the target?"

ME: "I ignored the pain."

HER: "So what should I do?"

ME: "Buy a gun with less recoil ... or ignore the pain."

HER: "But this one cost me over $600!"

ME: "The gun shop will probably give you $400 for it."

She was neither happy nor impressed with my wisdom.

Make sure you can handle the recoil before you buy a specific handgun. If you don't, then you could be losing a lot of money. I recommend that you go to a shooting range where they have rentals. If you're new to pistol shooting, go ahead and start out with a .22 caliber until you become proficient with the basics of marksmanship. Then move up in caliber and keep going until you find the highest caliber that you can accurately and safely control.

Some people will have to carry a .22 caliber because of physical limitations such as arthritis, carpal tunnel, or just general weakness in the wrists and hands. That's okay. Just do the best you can with what you have. Remember the number one rule to a gunfight is "Bring a gun!"

I used to shoot a .40 caliber, but have since changed to a 9 millimeter. Part of this is age. As a person grows older, they lose muscle mass. This makes it more difficult to accurately make successive shots. With the 9 millimeter I can maintain my accuracy after the first shot, because the recoil and muzzle flip isn't as pronounced.

Whatever caliber you choose, you should be able to maintain accuracy as you rapid-fire into the center of exposed mass.

Size

In the selection of a handgun for personal protection, "size matters." The size of the gun has to fit your hands. I've seen large men come to the range with small pocket guns like the Smith and Wesson Bodyguard in .380 caliber, and they had trouble hitting the target. Conversely, I've seen women come to the range shooting a full-frame Glock and have a similar problem with accuracy.

In a gunfight, you have to be able to proficiently run your gun with speed and precision. First off, tiny guns are not easy to shoot. Many beginners will come to class with these tiny guns, touting their compactness. That's true. Tiny guns are a joy to carry. On the other hand, tiny guns are a pain in the butt to shoot. The lighter the gun the more recoil you're going to feel. Here's why.

> A heavy gun will absorb more recoil than a light gun.

When the gun goes off, it produces a lot of energy. The first energy is used to send the bullet down the barrel, but there is energy left over. That leftover energy is used to complete the reloading cycle in the semi-automatic pistol. And any energy left after that is absorbed by the weight and mass of the gun. With small guns, there is leftover energy even after that, which has to be absorbed by your hands. Sometimes that hurts. The smaller the gun the more it hurts. The smaller and weaker your hands, the more pain you can feel. Those are the general rules.

Another potential problem is lack of dexterity. Very large hands and fingers find it difficult to do things like racking the slide or reloading the magazine when the parts of the gun are so small. I've seen big men on the line shooting a tiny gun that is literally swallowed up by the size and bulk of their hands.

> Select a handgun that feels good in your hand, with a natural point of aim.

To the other extreme, I've seen people shooting a full framed pistol where they cannot do even the most basic of tasks like pulling back on the slide or dropping the magazine. Your hands must have enough strength to easily pull back the slide and release it so the gun goes into battery. (That is, a loaded round is in the chamber and capable of firing.)

Semi-auto vs Revolver

This is a big one, and a bit of a debate in some self-defense circles, so I'm going to tell you the strengths and weaknesses of both revolvers and semi-automatics.

Revolver Strengths - Revolvers are inherently safe, reliable and dependable. Almost every time you pull the trigger they will go bang. After 16 years of teaching over 5,000 students to carry concealed, I've had only two revolvers malfunction on the range. One was brand new and defective from the factory. The second was fifty years old and never been cleaned. But, in general, they don't malfunction.

Revolvers are simpler than semi-autos, with fewer moving parts and less things to break. They are less complicated because they possess fewer bells and whistles like safety mechanisms, magazine release buttons and slide lock levers.

Some people like the long, hard trigger press of a revolver because it builds in a certain amount of safety, making it more difficult for them to press the trigger. However, despite the long, hard trigger press, don't assume that your child cannot pull the trigger on your revolver simply because it has a long pull and higher poundage. Children have loads of time and are smarter and stronger than you think.

> Revolvers are simple, but semi-autos have more firepower.

Revolver Weaknesses - The biggest downside to revolvers is their lack of stopping power. Most of the popular self-defense revolvers will have a five-shot capacity. And don't be fooled into thinking that you can reload quickly and easily under the stress of a gunfight. You are not Jerry Miculek. (Search for his videos on YouTube.) It takes thousands of hours to become proficient at reloading a revolver under stress. If you choose a revolver, just count on getting the job done with five shots or less.

Semiautomatic Strengths - The big deal here is firepower. Instead of a five or six-shot cylinder, you're going to have a magazine with a capacity of six to nineteen rounds. Plus, you will be able to reload much faster during a gunfight, provided you've practiced. Also, the grip is different on semi-autos vs revolvers. Some like the revolver grip while others like the semi-auto grip. The only way for you to know for sure is to try shooting both and compare.

> **Most semi-auto malfunctions can be prevented.**

Semi-automatic Weaknesses - Of course, the big downside of semi-automatics is the potential for malfunction during the reloading sequence. Having a failure to fire or a jam during a firefight is a complication that is difficult to overcome. That's the bad news. The good news is that, in my experience, most semi-auto malfunctions can be prevented with a little training and routine maintenance on your firearm.

Many malfunctions are caused by a limp wrist. The gun must have a steady, stable and strong shooting platform to push against while it's firing. The firing sequence goes like this.

1. The trigger is pressed.

2. The firing pin comes forward and hits the primer.

3. The primer ignites creating a small fire.

4. The fire ignites the propellant which burns, creating gas and pressure.

5. The gas and pressure push the bullet out the barrel.

6. The excess gas and pressure is channeled to the rear.

7. The slide moves to the rear, compressing the slide spring and ejecting the empty brass.

8. Once the slide reaches the rear, the compressed slide spring pushes the slide back forward.

9. As the slide moves forward, it pushes the next live round from the magazine, up the ramp and into the chamber.

That entire sequence takes but a fraction of a second. If, at any time during that sequence, you bend your wrist or absorb the recoil in any way, the gun can jam.

So the key to preventing malfunctions is to maintain good shooting position, giving the gun that stable shooting platform to push against. Now, of course there are other things that can cause a malfunction.

A weak magazine spring can cause a failure to feed the next round up into the chamber. When you have trouble with this, simply try a different magazine. If that fixes the problem, then replace the spring on the defective magazine or throw the magazine away.

Sometimes the magazine is not fully locked into place, and this will also cause a failure to feed, because the next live round isn't high enough to be shoved into the chamber. That's why on a malfunction procedure, we first tap the bottom of the magazine to ensure that it's fully seated.

> Keep your gun properly cleaned to help avoid malfunctions.

Weak ammo can also cause a malfunction. If there's not enough propellant in the round, then it lacks the energy to complete the reloading sequence. This is more common with those who reload their own ammo.

But again, all these weaknesses can be overcome by practice, training and regular maintenance. You have to decide how much work you're willing to put into it. If you're never going to practice, then you should consider buying a revolver for its simplicity and ease of use. But I recommend that you practice as much as possible whether you choose a revolver or a semi-automatic.

Trigger Press

Before buying a pistol, you should make sure you can easily press the trigger with either hand. It's not unusual to have people on the range who have extreme difficulty pressing the trigger one-handed. We practice shooting one-handed, because there are times in your life when one hand will be busy; for example, pushing back a loved one or pushing away your attacker. You could also be in a situation where one hand is out of commission, either having been shot during the course of the firefight or injured previously in your day-to-day life. Many new shooters aren't aware of this problem.

> Select a handgun that feels good in your hand, with a natural point of aim.

And now a word about trigger press and accuracy. In general, the lighter the trigger press, the more accurate the gun will be. If you have to struggle to press the trigger all the way to the rear, then you will likely torque the front sight to the left or right. This can be a problem with some of the less expensive guns and also with some of the self-defense revolvers. They tend to have a long, hard trigger press.

I recall the first national shooting school I went to. I had practiced on my own and thought I was pretty good. Then, on the day of reckoning, I was on the line and noticed that most of the other students were better shots than I. I redoubled my efforts to be accurate, but was quickly frustrated. Finally, the guy next to me pulled me off to the side and said, "You want to know why I'm shooting better than you?" I said, "Yes, of course." He told me to use his pistol on the next course of fire.

I was amazed at the difference in accuracy by going from a twelve-pound-trigger press to a five-pound trigger press. That one, small change cut the size of my bullet group in half.

WARNING

Be careful with modifications to your carry pistol. Lightening the trigger press makes your gun more accurate, but it also increases the potential for a negligent discharge. Most good self-defense semi-autos have about a five and a half pound trigger press from the factory, and that should be sufficient to maintain good tactical accuracy.

A Word about Gun Stores

I highly recommend that you already know which gun you want to buy before visiting the gun store. You should never walk into the gun shop and admit that you don't know what you want. If you do that, you might just walk out with a gun with the highest profit margin or the gun that the store clerk "feels" is the best one for you. (All gun salesmen have personal preferences, opinions and biases.) Once you've done all your homework and test fired a selection of handguns, go to the gun store and look at what's in the gun case. If you've decided to buy a 9 millimeter full frame, then have the clerk bring up each gun that meets your criteria. Then pick up each gun, one at a time, and get your regular shooting grip. If the gun feels like the ball glove you had when you were a kid, then it's a good candidate to be your concealed carry gun. As a further test, pull up the gun and look down the sights. If the sights

> Decide which gun you want "before" going to the gun store.

are lined up without having to make adjustments, then that's a gun you can use under stress successfully in a gunfight.

Here's why I say that. Do you remember the ball glove you had when you were a kid, how good it felt, how it molded to fit your hand when you used it and sweat on it? Your handgun won't mold to fit your hand no matter how much you use it or sweat on it. It's not made of leather; it's made of metal, wood and plastic. In a gunfight, within 10 feet, you are likely to use unsighted fire. If the sights don't line up naturally, then you'll miss your adversary while performing unsighted fire. This is called "natural point of aim" and is very important in select-ing a pistol for personal defense. (This is discussed in length in chapter 9 when learning about unsighted fire.)

NOTE

It's very important that you research local gun stores be-fore going there. Ask your shooting friends about the service. Are they knowledgeable? Is their primary interest fitting you with the "right" gun for your needs.

Summary

At best, selecting a personal defense carry gun is difficult and full of compromises. There is no perfect carry gun for you or anyone else. Many of the mistakes I've seen in firearm selection could have been avoided simply by shooting the gun before buying it. I recommend you shoot several calibers and sizes of guns before settling on one. You'll have to rent the guns from a shooting range or go shooting with a friend and try out their guns.

CAUTION

When you try out guns that are new to you, first run through an operations check. Make sure you know how all the mechanisms work, like the mag release, safety, slide lock lever, etc.

You can also go online and read reviews by professionals in the industry who have shot and tested the guns independent from their manufacturer.

Things to Remember

1. Shoot the highest caliber you can safely and accurately control.

2. Don't let someone else choose the right gun for you. Only you can do that.

3. Take the time to research the different makes and models of guns available.

4. Be sure to shoot the model of gun you want prior to purchase. (You wouldn't buy a car without test driving it.)

5. Make sure you can operate the gun, e.g., rack the slide, press the trigger, and engage safety mechanisms prior to buying.

Helpful Resources

www.gundigest.com

www.gunsandammo.com

www.uscca.com

Gun Digest's Choosing a Handgun for Self Defense eShort: Learn how to choose a handgun for concealed carry self-defense. (Concealed Carry eShorts) Kindle Edition

Chapter 8

In this chapter you will learn the following:

- The two basic modes of carry.
- The advantages and disadvantages of all types of carry.
- The proper and safe way to draw your firearm from concealment.

8

The Method of Carry

I REMEMBER WHEN I FIRST STARTED carrying concealed over sixteen years ago, my instructor told me that a year from now I would have a box of holsters that I never used. He was referring to selecting the method of carry, and that I would buy many holsters, try them out, and, for whatever reason, decide that holster wasn't for me. He was mostly right, although it took me two years, because I was on a fixed income.

I remember buying my first shoulder holster and thinking, "Wow! This is so cool! It's just like detectives in the movies." I paid a good price for that Galco rig and carried it for several days before someone asked me why my left breast was bulging out. I looked in the mirror and agreed that it looked kind of strange. I tried out several other options before finally settling, for the most part, on strongside hip carry. Even now I toy with other modes of carry. Rob Pincus seems to like an inside the waistband holster in the appendix position. Trying that out is on my list of things to do as well.

The point is, you may not get it right on the first try, so don't get discouraged. If at first you don't succeed, try, try again. Later on you can give those extra holsters away to friends you convert to the concealed carry lifestyle.

> There are two types of carry: on-body and off-body.

Holsters are manufactured with various materials such as leather, plastic and nylon. (Sometimes a combination of materials.) Some people swear by leather, while others prefer plastic or nylon. You won't know what you like best until you try it for yourself.

By now you may have figured out that carrying a concealed pistol for personal protection is a pretty serious thing. It's not just an accessory, it's a way of life that must be constantly improved upon. So, with that in mind, let's get at it.

In general, there are two types of carry: on-body and off-body.

On-body Carry

I define on-body carry as any method where the gun is physically attached to your body in some way. As such, it would be impossible to walk away from the gun without removing some type of garment, belt, holster or strap from your body. This is one of the most common methods of carry among men, and there are many ways to do it. Most people carry on their strong side (right side for right handed people and left side for left-handers.) Let's list out some of the methods of on-body carry along with a small description as well as their advantages and disadvantages of each method.

Hip Holster

The hip holster can be carried either strong or weak side, but it is always attached to your waist in some manner, usually by a belt. If you carry it weak side, then you'll have to draw the gun from across your body instead of moving straight down to your holster. Both are good, but you need to be aware that weak side is a longer drawstroke and will take longer for you to reach the gun, draw it and put the gun in play.

Advantage - This is a fast method of drawing from your holster as the draw stroke is much shorter.

Disadvantage - In order to conceal the gun you must wear an extra layer of clothing over it. This can be uncomfortable in hot climates.

CAUTION

With any type of cross draw, you may be indexing your hand or arm as you draw. Be very careful that your finger is off the trigger until you are on target and ready to shoot.

The holster will be either a belt-slide holster or a paddle holster. On a belt-slide holster, the belt will slide through slits cut into the leather or polymer holster. There will be a little play where the holster can slide along your waist on the belt. Try to always keep the holster in the same place as this can screw up your draw if the holster moves around too much. With a paddle holster, the holster doesn't at-

> Strong-side hip carry is a popular method allowing for a fast draw.

tach to the belt itself, it simply slips over it. The paddle is against your body with the belt and pants between the inside and outside of the holster. The paddle holster can be removed from your body without unholstering the gun. This is an advantage if you have to take the gun off to store it inside your vehicle or a gun safe.

CAUTION

Never use a holster that allows the trigger to be partially or fully exposed while inside it. These holsters are dangerous as they allow you to fire the gun while it is still holstered.

Some holsters have retention features which make it more difficult for your attacker to disarm you. These can be in the form of leather straps with snaps, a button to push before drawing, while others force you to push down on the gun before it is released. Some holsters may have more than one retention device. Be aware that while these retention features add a level of safety, they also slow down

> **Your carry belt should be wide enough and strong enough to support your gun's weight.**

your draw. As in everything else with concealed carry, you are constantly compromising to gain one advantage while sacrificing some other advantage.

NOTE ON BELTS

Make sure the belt is a strong one, either thick top-grain leather or nylon or canvas webbing. It should be specifically designed for concealed carry, as the weight of the gun will put a lot of stress on the belt. Also, make sure the belt is wide enough to support the holster and secure it in place so it doesn't slide or cant back and forth.

Outside the Waistband (OWB)

OWB is a holster, attaching to your belt, which resides outside the waist of your pants. The gun is protruding off your body. It is more difficult to conceal but allows for the fastest draw stroke for most people.

Advantages - This is the fastest draw method for most people. The gun is very accessible as it rides outside and clear of the belt and pants.

Disadvantages - It is bulky as the gun extends out past your body. You can't wear tight shirts over it without people seeing the bulk of the gun. You may bump the gun into door frames or even the heads of smaller children. (How do I know? Ask my kids.)

Inside the Waistband (IWB)

IWB is a holster, attaching to your belt, which resides inside the waist of your pants. So the gun is close to your body. It is much easier to conceal and still allows for a fairly smooth and quick draw.

> There are advantages and disadvantages to all types of carry.

Advantages - This makes the gun easier to conceal as the lower half of the gun is inside your pants. This works especially well if you're forced to wear a jacket and tie each day.

Disadvantages - The bulk of the gun requires your pants to be a larger size than normal, usually a 2 to 4 inch increase in the waist size. It may take some people longer to draw from IWB, especially if your belly extends out past your waistline.

Shoulder Rig

Shoulder rigs can be made of heavy leather, or nylon reinforced with leather. Be aware that heavier guns require leather with stronger nylon in order to give the gun adequate strength and support. For very light guns, there are all-nylon rigs that strap around your chest and secure with Velcro.

Advantages - This allows for deep concealment and a fairly fast draw.

Disadvantages - You are forced to draw across your body. You are also forced to wear another layer of clothing to conceal the gun.

Tactical Compression Shirts

Tactical Compression Shirts are made of stretchy nylon, like UnderArmor, with pockets by the shoulder that are used for small and light pistols. 511 Tactical makes a very nice concealed carry shirt,and it does well for its purpose. Just be aware that is doesn't adequately support the larger, heavier pistols.

> The deeper the concealment, the longer it takes to draw your gun.

Advantages - These are great for deep concealment. Your gun is very secure deep inside the pockets.

Disadvantages - As with any UnderArmor type of material, the shirt compresses against your skin fairly tight. Some people who have extra body weight may find it uncomfortable. Again, it is limited to smaller guns. You will also find that your draw is much slower when carrying in a tactical compression shirt.

Concealed Carry Vest

Concealed carry vests are sometimes called tactical vests. They have hidden pockets on the crossdraw side. They close with Velcro and they even have holsters secured inside with

Velcro pocket. They look a lot like fishing vests. They are loaded with pockets and extra storage compartments. Some say they look military in appearance.

Advantages - There are tons of pockets in these vests that give you plenty of storage area for extra magazines, flashlights, wallets, and anything else you want to stuff in there.

Disadvantages - The vest tends to slump to one side because of the weight of the gun. Some people offset that by weighting down the offside with other equipment. This is not a fancy vest, and will draw attention in even a semi-formal environment. Outside the rural environment, it will scream "tactical!"

Ankle Holsters

Ankle holsters are usually made of a combination of materials such as nylon, leather and Velcro. They are attached to the ankle by Velcro straps or leather and buckles. They are sometimes used by law enforcement to secure a back-up gun. They work very well with a 5-shot lightweight revolver.

> Ankle holsters are worn on the inside of your weak-side ankle.

Advantages - This method gets the gun off your waist and into a position that doesn't interfere with some work and motions that people go through frequently. It doesn't require additional clothing to conceal, provided you have long pants. This is an option that provides deep concealment.

Disadvantages - Ankle holsters will not support large frame handguns as most people have skinny ankles. The draw from an ankle holster is clumsy and slow, requiring you to drop down to one knee and pull up the pant leg. This process of dropping to one knee can be a severe tactical disadvantage as it limits your ability to move and escape.

Fanny Packs

Fanny packs are usually made of nylon or canvas. They are bags attached to a belt which goes around your waist and secures with some type of buckle. They usually contain additional compartments for storage.

> Never carry a gun in your pocket without a safe pocket holster.

Advantages - Fanny packs can also provide storage for your identification, cell phone, an extra magazine and other small personal items. They allow you to wear any clothing you want. This is especially nice in extreme cold or hot weather.

Disadvantages - Fanny packs are not common, especially at semi-formal to formal events and will appear out of place there. People who are familiar with concealed carry will assume the pack contains a pistol. The pack can be bulkier than a holster.

Pocket Holsters

Some people prefer to carry their gun inside their pants or jacket pocket. This is a very convenient way to carry, but the gun must be secure in order to be safe. The trigger must also be protected to avoid shooting yourself with your own gun. The pocket holster may have a large boot-shaped foot at the bottom to secure it in place. Many are made of suede leather or another sticky fabric to keep the holster from rotating in your pocket.

WARNING

Never carry a pistol inside a loose pocket. The gun may rotate with the muzzle pointing up. When you reach into the pocket to draw, you may press the trigger causing death or serious bodily injury.

Advantages - This is great for small guns and incredibly convenient. You can still wear whatever you want and no extra layer of clothing is required. It is possible to safely have your hand on the grip of the gun while walking in public places.

Disadvantages - The pocket must be large enough to accommodate the bulk of the gun plus the holster. The draw tends to be slower than some methods.

Other Methods

There are a lot of other methods of carry, most of which are not widely used, but which some people really like. I'll list them here as a reference and you can look them up online for more information.

> There are many methods of carry, but none are perfect.

Thunderwear - A nylon, elastic girdle that is worn over your undergarment with a built-in holster in front.

Flash Bang - A holster that attaches to a bra in the center front. These are becoming increasingly more popular among women carriers.

Belly Band - A wide elastic band that straps around the waist with a pocket for a holster.

Sticky Holster - Usually made of nylon or neoprene, it tucks inside the waistband and is held in place by the pressure of your body pushing against your waistband. This holster can be an excellent starter holster as it is inexpensive and allows you to carry in any location around your waist.

Corset Holsters - A holster attached to a close-fitting under-garment made of a stretch fabric such as nylon or neoprene.

Garter Holster - Made of nylon or neoprene and attaches to the thigh of the carrier.

Off-body Carry

I define off-body carry as any method of carry where the gun is not physically attached to the body and where you can set the mode of carry down and walk away from it. This is one of the most popular methods of carry for women, as it allows them to wear any clothing they like. The big advantage to off-body carry is convenience. The potential downside is safety. Here are some popular modes of off-body carry.

> It's no longer a purse - it's a gun.

Concealed Carry Purses

This is a popular method of carry for women. Purses come in all shapes, colors, materials and sizes, with many pockets for storage. Most concealed carry purses will have a secret compartment near the rear, and some have actual holsters inside to fit your model of gun. Others will have a locking mechanism on the zipper compartment where the gun is stored.

Advantages - Ease of use and convenience are a big plus with concealed carry purses. Women are very fashion conscious and this frees them to wear any clothing they like.

Disadvantages - The gun can be put down on a table or in a shopping cart and left unattended. This has severe, potential safety ramifications.

WARNING

Any type of off-body carry can have potential life-threatening dangers, especially if you have small children in your home. Kids love to get into Mommy's purse. If you carry your gun in your purse, it ceases to be a purse, and must now be viewed as a gun. The purse must always be under your direct, physical control and never left on a table, counter or anywhere accessible to other people. As soon as the gun leaves your shoulder or hands, it must go directly into the gun safe.

> **Never set your gun down and walk away from it.**

Briefcases

Some people prefer to carry in a brief case as they travel throughout the day and at their workplace. The same safety measures must be taken with briefcases as with purses. They are very stylish, have holsters inside as well as locks to keep them there.

Advantages - Ease of use and convenience are a big plus with briefcases. They also allow for storage of extra magazines and pepper spray. It's also possible to line your briefcase with Kevlar as added protection should a gun fight ensue.

Disadvantages - The briefcase can be put down on a table or a desk and left unattended. This has severe, potential safety ramifications.

Drawing from Concealment

Drawing from concealment can be dangerous if not done properly. Of course, you should follow all the rules of safety while drawing your pistol. It's very important that you keep your finger off the trigger until the gun is on target and you've made the decision to shoot. If you want to see what happens when you break the rules, do an online search for "people shooting themselves in the butt." Only then will you fully understand the seriousness of drawing a loaded firearm.

When first learning to draw from concealment, you should start out slowly and do it by the numbers. Always use an unloaded or training firearm when practicing your draw. (Later, when you are better trained you can add live ammo. But don't rush it. Take the time and about 3,000 perfect repetitions before you go live.) Let's go over the steps of drawing from concealment in detail.

1. Clear the clothing. If you have a shirt or jacket, open it in the front and then swipe your gun hand back in one strong motion. Use the edge of your hand to push the garment clear of the gun.

If your shirt is not open in front, then clear the clothing by pulling the shirt up with your offhand. As you are clearing the clothing, your offhand should move to your sternum and press flatly against your chest. Alternately, you can still draw one handed when your shirt is closed in front by running the thumb on your strong hand up the pants seam until it reaches the shirt and lifts it upward and out of the way.

CAUTION

It is very important to clear the fabric completely so as not to interfere with the next step. Failure to clear the clothing could result in an unintentional discharge, causing injury or death.

Remember, the grip you draw from, is the grip you'll shoot with.

NOTE

You will naturally drop your center of gravity and spread your feet shoulder-width apart as soon as you recognize the deadly encounter. This is done simultaneously as you move your offhand to your sternum and clear the clothing.

2. Grip the Firearm. Your gun hand should travel straight down to the gun and grasp it firmly on the grip. The webbed portion of your hand between the thumb and forefinger should be centered firmly on the backstrap of the gun. Grip and squeeze the gun, wrapping your three outside fingers around the frontstrap of the grip. The grip should be firm, strong and not hampered by clothing.

3. Draw the Firearm. After releasing any retention mechanisms, pull the gun directly upward until the muzzle clears the top of the holster. The gun should still be pointed straight down, but not at your leg. It is paramount that your trigger finger remain off the trigger and outside the trigger guard along the slide or cylinder.

4. Rotate the Firearm. Rotate the gun ninety degrees so it is pointed straight forward in front of you. The gun should still be at your side and directly above the holster. Again, the finger is off the trigger and outside the trigger guard along the slide or cylinder.

CAUTION

At this point, if the threat merits it, you are in a physical position to discharge the firearm. Make sure the slide on the semi-auto does not come back and hit your chest as this could cause a malfunction.

5. Join the gun with the offhand. Move your gun to the center of your chest and join the gun with your offhand to form a two-handed grip. Again, the finger is off the trigger and outside the trigger guard along the slide or cylinder.

6. Move the gun forward into shooting position. Thrust the gun directly forward with force and strength. Your arms should be locked and the elbows not bent. Your shoulders should be moved forward as far as they can go to lock the

position in place. When you are ready to shoot, place your finger on the trigger and press to the rear.

7. Recover and reholster. Once the threat is gone, you should move your gun back to the high-ready position (the position you had in step 5, the join position.) Then move your head from side to side and to the rear as you scan for other possible threats. Once you determine there are no other threats, you may reholster your pistol, being careful that your finger is off the trigger.

Summary

There are many different methods of concealed carry, and I've described only the major ones and mentioned some of the other more esoteric modes of carry. The primary things to consider in carrying concealed are safety and accessibility. To a lesser degree consider concealability and apparel. As with selecting the best personal defense gun, there is no perfect method of carry. Everything is a series of compromises.

Helpful Training Courses

Concealed Carry and Home Defense Fundamentals
United States Concealed Carry Association (USCCA)

Basic Firearm Safety Course
The National Rifle Association (NRA)

Basic Pistol Course
The National Rifle Association (NRA)

Personal Protection in the Home Course
The National Rifle Association (NRA)

Personal Protection Outside the Home Course
The National Rifle Association (NRA)

Things to Remember

1. You may have to try many methods of carry before you find the holster you want.

2. Be careful with off-body carry. Treat your purse or briefcase like you treat your gun.

3. Retention holsters add a measure of safety, but also slow down your draw.

4. Drawing from concealment, when not done properly, is very dangerous.

5. Start out your practice using an unloaded gun or a practice training gun.

6. It requires 3,000 perfect repetitions to ingrain muscle memory.

7. Start your practice using the step-by-step method, then smooth it out.

PART III
THE GORY DETAILS

Chapter 9

In this chapter you will learn the following:

- Where to aim on the human body.
- All about psychological stops.
- All about physical stops.
- When to use a challenge command.
- All about penetration.
- The basics of sighted and unsighted fire.

> *"The history of gun fighting for more than a century has shown that the person who lands the first solid hit will usually win the confrontation."*
>
> —*Dave Spaulding, International Trainer., Handgun Combatives, Inc."*—

9

Stopping the Threat

W E'VE ALREADY TALKED ABOUT shooting to stop the threat, but, let's face it, many times the threat can only be stopped by causing massive tissue damage and blood loss. So, let's take some time now to talk about the different ways to stop the threat. In general, there are two types of stops: they are the psychological stop and the physical stop.

Psychological Stop

A psychological stop is when you point the gun at the attacker, he sees the gun, and then flees. In a psychological stop, it doesn't matter what caliber of gun you're shooting. The bottom line is this: "The bad guy doesn't want to be shot, so he leaves." In some cases you may have to shoot before he flees the scene. That's okay. If you even make a superficial hit he is

125

> **In a psychological stop, the bad guy doesn't want to fight.**

leaving simply because he's not psychologically prepared to participate in a gun fight. Psychological stops are a good thing. You didn't have to kill the attacker, and they didn't kill you. But here's the problem: psychological stops occur roughly forty percent of the time. That means six out of ten attackers will keep coming after you even after you draw your firearm. For those people, you need something special.

NOTE

For more information on the statistics regarding psychological vs physical stops, refer to the study done by Greg Ellifritz. You can find it at the website for Buckeye Firearms Association.

(www.buckeyefirearms.org/alternate-look-handgun-stopping-power)

Physical Stop

When you have a determined attacker, you'll be forced to make a physical stop. That is, you'll have to take away something he needs in order to continue the fight. One of those things is oxygen. There are two types of physical stops; they are as follows:

1. Hydraulic Stop

In a hydraulic stop, you are trying to lower the blood pressure to the point where the attacker bleeds out. Without oxygen to the brain, the attacker loses consciousness and dies. The blood is the way our body transports oxygen from the lungs to the brain. If you punch enough holes in his body, the blood will drain out and eventually he'll pass out and die. Depending on the effectiveness of your shots, it can take a matter of seconds, or a matter of minutes or even hours. In a hydraulic stop, you want to stop them in a matter of seconds, not minutes.

In a hydraulic stop, think of the heart simply as a hydraulic pump, whose primary job is to pump oxygenated blood to the brain and the other organs and extremities. A heart shot is a good thing. If you hit your attacker in the heart, he is almost certain to die. But here's the problem, at any given point in time, there are 15 to 20

> There are 2 types of physical stops: electrical and hydraulic.

seconds worth of oxygen in the average brain. So, even if you blow up the heart, the attacker can maintain consciousness for 15 to 20 seconds. From a practical standpoint, that means he can return fire for a long period of time. So, just because he's going to die, doesn't guarantee that you're going to live. How many shots can he get off in 15 seconds? He can unload the magazine. Even though he's going to die, that doesn't mean he can't take you with him. That means we shoot to stop the threat. If the gun is still in his hand and it's pointed in your direction, then the threat is ongoing and you must continue making good stopping hits.

2.   Electrical Stop

Roughly seventy-five percent of the time, an electrical stop results in immediate incapacitation. An electrical stop is defined as any hit to the brain or the upper spine. That sounds good. You hit them in the brain; they go down; and you live. It's like that electrical panel in your basement. It has a lever on the side; that's called the main breaker. You pull the lever down, and all electrical activity in the house stops. That's a good thing, right? But here's the problem with that. Head shots are really tough to make and incredibly tough to make under stress. In addition to that, the head tends to move more than the torso, and moving targets are tough to hit. The head turns and the angle changes, thus, making you adjust your aim under desperate circumstances while your heart is racing at 120 plus beats per minute.

The upper spine is the same way. It's a skinny target, requiring adequate penetration from the front before taking effect. Now, don't get me wrong, it's an incredibly effective shot. If you're a hunter and you've spine shot a deer, you know what I'm talking about. They don't run away, they simply drop straight down, and it's a pitiful sight to see.

Shot Placement

My students always ask me "So where do I aim?" Well, in the unfortunate event that you are left with no choice other than to use deadly force, you should aim for the center of exposed mass. Now, in most cases that will be the sternum. Of course there are rare cases where it could be the center of the head or hip or any other body part that happens to be protruding out past the cover, but, in general, in the vast majority of scenarios, center of exposed mass will be the sternum.

> In general, we shoot for the center of exposed mass.

Upper Chest Shots

Anatomically speaking, there's a lot of good targets in the upper chest region. You have the heart, the lungs, the superior vena cava and the aorta. (See figure below.) And, if you shoot high it gets even better. Up higher you have the windpipe, the jugular, and of course, the spine is always lurking in the background, provided you get adequate penetration. The sternum is a very forgiving shot. If you shoot a foot high, then you hit the brain. If you shoot a foot low, then you're in the pelvic region. However, if you're a foot to the right or left, then you've missed the target altogether. It's important to stay on the vertical line between the brain and the tailbone. If you stay on that vertical line, then your chances of making a critical hit are enhanced.

> In general, the 1st person to score a critical hit wins.

The first person to score a critical hit usually wins the gun fight. A critical hit is defined as any hit to the central nervous system or a major organ. Once you score a critical hit, the attacker's ability to continue attacking begins to degrade, thus, giving you the edge and enhancing your chances of survival. Of course, just because you make one good hit, doesn't guarantee you'll survive. So, as always, you continue to shoot until the threat stops.

Trachea

Spine

Aorta

Heart

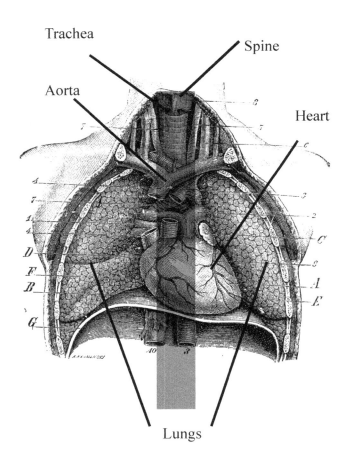

Lungs

Making the Upper Chest Shot

Pelvic girdle shots (Mechanical Stops)

There was a study done by Dave Spaulding of Handgun Combatives Inc., where he shot bullets of varying calibers into human skeletons (yes, they were already dead). I was in a class taught by Dave when he spoke of this. He was expecting the pelvic girdle to shatter, but was surprised to see that it did not. The bullets simply left holes in the bone. The only time massive damage resulted was when the bullets hit the ball joints in the hip. This caused him to conclude that when you shoot for the pelvic girdle, you should aim for the pockets on the attacker's pants, thus, getting good hits and potentially shattering the hip joints. (See figure below.) That won't kill them right away, but will severely degrade

> On pelvic girdle shots, aim for the pants pockets to hit the ball joints.

their mobility. That's a great edge in a fire fight. I also asked Massad Ayoob as to the advisability of a pelvic girdle shot, and he pointed out that when fighting against someone with body armor this could be a good option as a lot of civilian grade body armor does not extend down past the waist line. This is done by design for comfort.

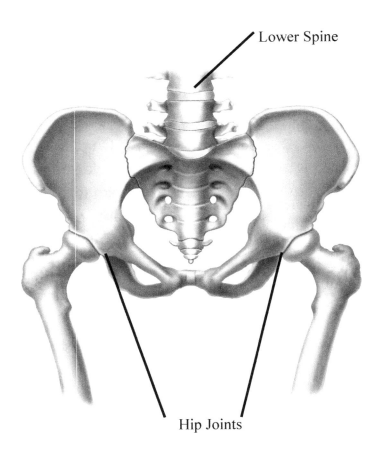

Lower Spine

Hip Joints

Making the Pelvic Girdle Shot

Head Shots

Let me be very clear about this. The vast majority of my civilian students will not be able to make an effective head shot during a deadly force encounter. We all hear stories about Navy SEALS and other Special Forces types who can do it, but they send thousands of rounds per week down the barrel. I don't know anyone personally who does that. In general, I teach my students to stick to the tried-and-true center of ex-

> Head shots are extremely effective, but very difficult to make.

posed mass shot, which typically will be the upper chest area. It's easier to hit consistently when under severe duress.

When a man is coming toward you full speed, the angles are changing nonstop. Even with the perfect angle, the attacker is facing you, giving you a clear shot at the ocu-

lar cavity; it's still almost an impossible shot to make under stress. The size of the kill zone is roughly a 3 by 5 index card. The point of aim is the eyes and bridge of the nose. And just for grins, consider this: the forehead is the thickest part of the skull. If the head is tilted back you're hitting an angled surface which may cause the bullet to glance upward, and not get through to vital tissue.

I still practice that shot myself, but only for a few scenarios:

1. Close quarters encounter - An example of this could be a mugging. I begin this drill by moving off the line as I draw. The first two shots are to the head as

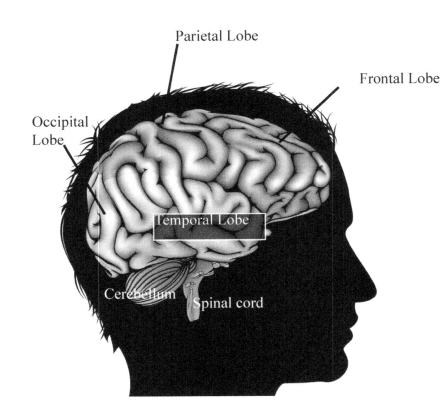

Making the Head Shot

I'm moving back at a diagonal. By the third shot I'm already moving down to the upper chest area.

2. Hostage scenario/extended firefight - Let's be honest. This hardly ever happens in the civilian world except in Hollywood. Most firefights last only a few seconds. Nonetheless, I practice shooting well-placed shots from behind cover just in case.

3. Body armor - Most bad guys don't wear body armor, but ... every once in a while they do. So, I practice head shots as well as pelvic shots just to maintain the proficiency.

Sights or No Sights?

There's always a debate among some instructors as to which is superior: sighted or unsighted fire? The answer of course is ... yes. I like them both. Let's go over the advantages and limitations of both, and then we'll talk about the "how to."

> You should practice both sighted and unsighted fire.

1. Unsighted Fire - This is sometimes called point shooting or instinctive shooting. This is based around eye-hand coordination and natural point of aim. When a baseball player throws a strike, he's not using sights. He burns a hole in the catcher's mitt with his eyes and then uses muscle memory to throw the ball as accurately as possible. The basic premise is, his hand, arm and shoulder work together to put the ball where his eyes are focused. And it works pretty good ... after tens of thousands

of repetitions. And, of course, natural talent in the form of good eye-hand coordination is a big help. Here are the up-sides of unsighted fire.

- You are able to shoot at a faster rate of fire, simply because you aren't taking the time to realign the sights after each recoil. When I point shoot, I can press the trigger as fast as I can, and the shots go where I want them to, provided my eyes are focused on the exact center of the target. This comes in handy when someone is trying to kill you.

- It is easier to shoot with both eyes open without having to line up sights. Shooting with both eyes open is superior from a tactical standpoint, because you have the ability to see the entire field of battle. It also aids in balance while moving and shooting. Try running with one eye closed. It's not easy.

- Most shootings occur in low-light conditions where it's often difficult to see your sights. With unsighted fire, you're not trying to see the sights. If you can see the outline and center mass of your assailant, then you can point and shoot effectively, provided you've put in the requisite practice time.

> **Take the time to learn your maximum effective range using unsighted fire.**

Here are the down sides to unsighted fire:

- Unsighted fire is less accurate at longer distances. In my advanced classes, I have my student stand five feet from the target. He points and shoots. If he hits the target, then he backs up a step and tries again. He repeats this process of shooting and moving back until reaching his maximum effective range without sights. That is, when he stops hitting the paper plate, he stops moving back. Then he practices at that range until he masters it. Then he can move another pace back, thereby, extending his maximum effective range. I have a few exceptional beginning students with a maximum effective range of thirty feet, but accuracy for most begins to degrade beyond ten feet. When I practice my tactical shooting, I'm point shooting within ten feet, and then I begin my transition to sights simply by moving the gun up in front of my eyes where they naturally acquire the sights.

> Sighted fire is more accurate at longer distances.

- Potentially the biggest downside to unsighted fire is this: some people can't do it very well. Obviously, you can improve even if you aren't gifted with exceptional eye-hand ability, but, let's face it, we are not all created equal. I consider myself to have average eye-hand coordination, but, with practice, I can stay on the upper chest region beyond twenty feet at a high rate of accurate fire. Now, don't get me wrong, I'm more accurate beyond twenty feet with sights. In my experience, very few people are more accurate without sights at these longer distances. However, the vast majority of shooters can become accurate enough to hit the upper chest region while moving at least out to a distance of ten feet.

2. Sighted fire - When using sights a beginner can get up and running in a single afternoon and be hitting the target with little to no experience, primarily because he has a reference point. He has the front

sight, rear sight, sight alignment and sight picture. With unsighted fire, it's more like flying by the seat of your pants. With sighted fire, you're flying with instruments.

Here are the advantages of sighted fire:

- Sighted fire can be extremely accurate, especially at longer ranges. I like to use sighted fire when I'm safely behind cover. Cover allows me to slow down and take well-placed, aimed shots.

Here are the limitations of sighted fire:

- Sight acquisition is difficult in low-light conditions.
- Sight acquisition is difficult while moving.
- Sight shooting has a slower rate of fire.

The basics of sighted fire

When first learning to shoot, it's obvious who understands sight alignment and who does not just by looking at their target. If you understand how to line up the sights, then your target will have holes in it. I know that sounds simplistic, but it's true. A picture is worth a thousand words, so make your sights look like the next figure, and you'll be on target.

Rear Sights

Front Sight

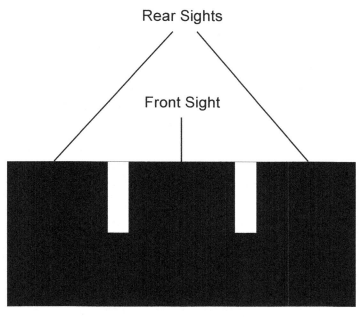

Notice that the front sight is perfectly aligned vertically and flush with both the left and right notches of the rear sight with equal amounts of daylight on either side.

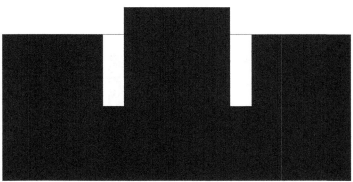

If the front sight is high, the shot will miss high.

If the front sight is low, the shot will miss low.

If the front sight is left, the shot will miss left.

If the front sight is right, the shot will miss right.

The general rule is this: the shot will always follow the front sight. As such, your eyes should always focus on the front sight. It's impossible for your eyes to focus on more than one object or distance at a time. The front sight should be in perfect, crisp focus and alignment. The rear sights should be a blur, and the target should be a blur. Then you take that perfect sight alignment and center it on the target. This is called sight picture.

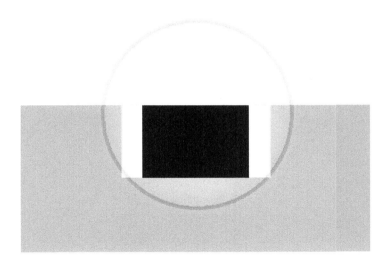

Notice that the front sight is perfectly aligned and flush with both the left and right notches of the rear sight with equal amounts of daylight on either side. The circular target is blurred as well as the notches of the rear sight. But the top of the front sight is exactly where you want the bullet to go.

If the sight alignment is off just a tiny bit, it will result in a miss. The greater the distance, the greater the miss. Bullets always travel in a straight line, so it's a matter of simple geometry, lines and angles as illustrated in the figure above. (X marks the bullseye.)

Trigger Control

In a Lethal Force Institute class with Bob Houzenga of Midwest Training Group (winner of six national shooting titles) Bob referred to the trigger as the heart of the beast. If you conquer the trigger, you conquer the beast. No matter how you phrase it, it is generally agreed that most accuracy is limited by how well you control the trigger. If you can learn to press the trigger slowly, smoothly and steadily, directly to the rear, without moving the front sight, then you are destined to be highly accurate. Of course, that's a really big "IF."

> The trigger is the heart of the beast. Conquer the trigger and conquer the beast.

The lighter and smoother the trigger, the more potential accuracy there is using sighted fire.

CAUTION

Be very careful about modifying your trigger press. Too light a trigger press, while more accurate, can be dangerous, especially when drawing from the holster under stress.

Follow Through

If you find yourself missing the target by a large distance, either high or low, then you may have a problem with follow through. This usually happens when people are afraid of the recoil. You press the trigger slow and steady to the rear, but then just before the gun goes off, you push forward on the pistol to counteract the recoil that will push back at you. (This can be caused by a tensing of the pectoral muscles.) This will cause the shot to go low. I've seen extreme cases where people have launched rounds into the dirt several feet in front of them.

In other cases, people start their trigger press, then just before it goes off, they pull their head to one side (bail out) and this makes the shot go high.

The fix for this is to make friends with the recoil. I tell my students to treat the gun like a nice, warm puppy. Then I pet the slide. (Yes, I know it's silly.) The gun will not hurt you so long as you stay behind the muzzle. In some cases shooters need to lessen the recoil because they physically are not able to control it because of strength issues. I've seen people with arthritis, carpal tunnel, or just plain weak hands and they need to go down in caliber. Sometimes you just need to desensitize yourself to the recoil by shooting over and over again until you're no longer bothered by it.

> Make friends with the recoil. It means the gun is working properly.

Summary

This chapter is not meant to be an exhaustive tutorial on how to shoot a pistol. I believe that is best done one-on-one with an experienced trainer on the range. You can learn only so much from books.

When it comes to shot placement, you should practice for the scenario in which you will most likely fight. (That is, the Dynamic Critical Incident.) For most of us, we'll be close, that is, contact distance to ten feet. Eighty percent of my personal practice is done at close distances while moving to cover. Most of the time I practice moving and shooting without using my sights. But once I get beyond my maximum effective unsighted shooting range, I transition to sights. Again, once I'm safely behind cover, I also transition to sights, thereby making more precise, well-placed stopping shots on the assailant.

Conclusion: Practice both sighted and unsighted fire. Become proficient using both methods and your chances of prevailing in a gunfight are greatly enhanced. Remember, you can survive a gunfight and be in a wheelchair for the rest of your life. You don't want to just "survive." You want to "WIN!"

Things to Remember

1. Most civilian shootings occur within 10 feet.

2. Learn from a competent professional how to safely move and shoot.

3. Practice shooting using both sighted and unsighted fire.

4. When using sighted fire, the shot will always follow the front sight.

5. Unsighted fire is superior at close distances.

6. When you reach your maximum effective range for unsighted fire, transition to your sights.

7. In most cases, shoot for the center of the upper chest area. This is the most forgiving, high-percentage shot.

Helpful Resources

Here are some great shooting schools, which I can personally recommend.

ICE Training (Rob Pincus)
www.icetraining.us

Midwest Training Group (Bob Houzenga)
www.midwesttraininggroup.net

Massad Ayoob Group (Massad Ayoob)
www. massadayoobgroup.com

Firearms Academy of Seattle, (Kathy Jackson)
www.firearmsacademy.com

Handgun Combatives, Inc, (Dave Spaulding)
www.handguncombatives.com

Canovi & Associates (Matt Canovi)
www.mattcanovi.com

Chapter 10

In this chapter you will learn the following:

- When am I justified in using deadly force?
- What is serious bodily injury?
- The standard rule of deadly force.
- The totality of the circumstances.
- How the legal system works.
- How to get competent legal help.

10
When Can I Shoot?

THERE YOU ARE IN THE PARKING garage. You've been working late, so it's dark, and you're all alone. As you near your car, a man steps out from behind a concrete pillar and lunges at you with a knife. Instinctively, you step to one side, narrowly escaping the knife as you draw your firearm. The man recovers, and you raise your gun and shoot multiple times into his upper chest. The man hesitates, looks at you with disbelief, then suddenly realizes he's about to die. He staggers and then falls to the pavement at your feet where he bleeds out quickly. His breathing becomes loud and choppy as the muscles in his throat begin to relax. And then he dies. You look down at the gun in your hand. Your gaze moves to the body at your feet. This is the moment you've been training and preparing for, all the while hoping to avoid it, but ... it seems different than you'd imagined it would be. But there is no denying the one, simple fact. Your life has changed forever.

Okay, that is a pretty bleak picture, but the fact remains you were attacked, and you did what you had to do to survive. That is, you took another human life. You've just committed homicide.

homicide (dictionary.com)
[hom-uh-sahyd]
noun
1. The killing of one human by another.

There are two types of homicide: criminal and justifiable. Criminal homicide can be classified as either murder or manslaughter.

murder - the killing of a human by another human with malice aforethought.

> The killing of one human by another is called homicide.

malice aforethought (dictionary.com) - a predetermination to commit an unlawful act without just cause or provocation.

According to these definitions, the man with the knife just tried to murder you. You committed homicide, but did you commit a crime? The answer is "no" because your actions were justified under the law.

How do I know when I am legally availed the use of deadly force?

That's an excellent question, and one you should be fluent in answering if you're going to carry a gun for personal defense. The problem is this: it's not always cut and dried, especially in the heat of the moment with all that adrenaline pumping. Things happen quickly in real life, and you probably won't have a lot of time to think it through. But here are the general guidelines to follow. But first a few disclaimers.

Disclaimer

I am not a lawyer. These are general guidelines to follow, but you should seek out the advice of a licensed and legal professional in your jurisdiction for a better and more thorough explanation of the law.

Disclaimer

Laws about the use of deadly force vary from jurisdiction to jurisdiction and are continually changing. Take the time and effort to research your jurisdiction as the law may be more or less strict where you live. Again - consult the best attorney you can afford.

So, the question at hand is "When can I shoot?" First, a short discussion. Let me make it clear that we don't "want" to shoot. If you're the type of personality that "wants" to shoot, and is looking for a reason to shoot, then do us all a favor and don't carry a gun. A firearm is a tool of last resort and should always be viewed as such, especially in self-defense applications.

> When you can safely retreat, you should avoid using deadly force.

Having said that, I can tell you the vast majority of my

students go to the opposite extreme. Some of them will go through mental and moral gymnastics trying to find a reason to not shoot. Determining when to shoot is a bit of a tightrope, and you can get in trouble with either extremes.

On the one end of the spectrum, if you take too long to determine deadly force is justified, you could end up face-down, dead in an alley. On the other, if you shoot too fast, before you are legally justified, you can end up in prison. So this is a very important topic to study and to be absolutely sure about.

> Make the best decision you can, but you won't always be certain.

But before we have this discussion, we need to define deadly force.

Deadly force - that ACTION known to create a SUBSTANTIAL RISK of causing death or serious bodily injury.

We all know what death is; it's pretty binary; you're either dead or alive, and those are the only two choices. But what is serious bodily injury?

Serious bodily injury - any injury that results in broken bones, stitches, permanent disfigurement, or substantial loss of consciousness.

NOTE

This could also include puncture wounds or anything else your attorney can prove to cause serious internal bleeding. For example, a ruptured kidney.

With that definition in mind, answer this question.

Is it reasonable to assume a man attacking you with a

152

tennis racket can inflict serious bodily injury?

Maybe. That brings in another factor. If you are attacked by a man wielding a tennis racket, and you use deadly force to defend yourself, the justification of use of deadly force may be determined on three separate occasions by three different people or groups.

1. The police officer responding to the scene will make a determination as to whether your action was justifiable under the laws of your jurisdiction. After researching the evidence, he'll make a determination. If he believes your actions were reasonable, then he may not take you to jail. If he believes your actions were not reasonable, then you'll

> The prosecutor will decide whether or not to charge you with a crime.

almost surely be arrested. Either way, the police officer will write up his report and send it on to the Prosecuting Attorney for consideration.

2. The Prosecutor will then make his determination: Were you justified in using deadly force? That is, would a reasonable person have done the same thing in the same circumstance. If the prosecutor believes your actions were reasonable, then no criminal charges will be filed. If he believes they were not justified, then he'll press criminal charges and you'll go to trial.

3. Once in the courtroom, the jury will listen to all the evidence and make the final determination on whether or not your use of deadly force was "reasonable." In short, "reasonable" will be defined as the combined intelligence of that jury.

It's important to note that sometimes innocent people go to prison, so take this very seriously.

The jury will be considering the "Totality of the Circumstances" to determine the reasonableness of your actions. Another name for this is "The Big Picture." Some of the factors they consider are as follows:

THE BIG PICTURE

Night vs Day - as a culture we are predisposed to be afraid of the dark. After all, in the dark we can't see danger coming and we feel more vulnerable because of it. We also know that criminals prefer the cover of darkness; that is, bad and dangerous things come out at night.

> The jury will decide if your action was reasonable.

Age, Physical ability, Size and Gender - In general, society gives more protection to our weakest members, and this is reflected in our legal system. Let's face it, the older we get the less able we are to defend ourselves against a physical threat. As we age we lose muscle mass, energy, vision, hearing, mental faculties, speed, and athletic ability. Many of my students are sixty and older, have artificial joints, back problems, arthritis, and a host of other ailments, all brought on by the normal course of aging. Size is also an issue. When a 300 pound body builder attacks a 100-pound woman, she will be more readily availed the use of deadly force than if she had attacked him. In short, he is capable of killing her with his bare hands, while she is not.

Weather conditions - Is it foggy, rainy, are the sidewalks covered with ice and slippery? That's an issue, because it reduces your ability to flee and could force you to fight to defend yourself in certain situations.

Ability of Attacker - Is the attacker an award winning Ultimate Fighting Championship (UFC) fighter? Is he a third degree black belt in karate? Does he have a history of violence? All of these things are factors, but you have to be able to document that you knew these things prior to the shooting incident.

Number of Attackers - This is a big one. Many people would agree that one person has a chance of fighting off a single attacker, and may not be forced to use deadly force. But add one, two or more attackers, and that changes. It's simply not reasonable to assume that a single person can successfully defend against a group of people trying to hurt or kill.

Weapons - Is the attacker using a deadly weapon against you? We all know that knives, firearms and ball bats can be used as deadly weapons. But what about tennis rackets, chairs, table legs, etc. It depends on the ability of the attacker with that particular weapon in that particular situation.

> The totality of circumstances is called "The Big Picture."

Unfamiliar Territory - We feel less secure in a strange town, because we don't know what places to avoid. This often happens when we have car trouble on vacation. We pull off the highway and find the streets lined with people staring at us. Why? Because you don't belong there. You are an anomaly.

Response time - Is the cavalry coming to save you? If so, will they get there in time? In some jurisdictions, in the middle of the night, it may take 30 minutes for the police to arrive. If so, then you're on your own.

Family and friends present - Are there people there who are able and willing to help you without the use of deadly force? If not, then you are the lone ranger. This adds to your feeling of vulnerability.

Anything else you can think of. - This is no joke. Some lawyers can be pretty creative in their defense or attack. Do you remember the OJ Simpson trial? In the end, the jury was asked to find the defendant not guilty based on the size of his hands. "If the glove doesn't fit you must acquit!"

Right about now your head is probably swimming, overwhelmed with all these potential factors. Here's the basic rule when determining whether use of deadly force is justified.

STANDARD RULE:

At the time you acted you must have HONESTLY and REASONABLY believed that you were in danger of being killed or seriously injured.

In addition to that:

The threat must be imminent (or immediate) and the suspect must have the ability, intent and opportunity and you must be in reasonable fear.

Let's break that down so all can understand it.

HONESTLY - The jury believes you. You're not lying, and the evidence supports you. You can't just pretend to be in fear. It has to be real.

REASONABLY - This means the jury came to the same conclusion that you did. That is, "A different person would have done the same thing in the same situation."

IMMINENT - The attack is going to happen right now. Not tomorrow, not 60 seconds from now. The attack is immediate and shall occur without a doubt.

ABILITY - The attacker must have the physical and men-

156

tal ability to cause you death or serious bodily injury. If you're 25 years old and you shoot a ninety-year-old woman for attacking you with her bare hands, I can't envision a case where you will not go to prison. She was not capable of killing you and you had other options like less than lethal force or just plain walking away.

INTENT - Do they really intend to do you harm? Can that be proved in a court of law? If they had no intention of hurting you, then you are not availed the use of deadly force. For example, they were just joking when they said, "I'm gonna stab you." If the witnesses present testify that the attacker had no intent, then you're in trouble.

> The attacker must have the ability, intent and opportunity.

OPPORTUNITY - A man who lives in Australia makes a death threat to you online. "I'm going to fly to America and kill you!" So you, being proactive, buy a plane ticket to Sidney, and meet him as he walks out of his apartment and gun him down. In court you say it was self-defense and you have the email to prove it. This will not work. You're going to prison, because the threat must be imminent and because the attacker must have the opportunity to commit the crime.

To sum it up, before you are availed the use of deadly force, *your attacker must have the ability to kill or seriously hurt you, the intention of killing or seriously hurting you and the opportunity to kill or seriously injure you.*

In addition to that, you must have *honestly and reasonably believed that he was about to kill you or cause serious bodily injury.*

Shooting in defense of a stranger

People always ask, Can I use deadly force to protect another innocent person? The answer is usually yes. Once again, this may vary from jurisdiction to jurisdiction. Make sure you consult with your local attorney who can brief you on the laws of your state. If you can't afford an attorney, look it up on the state attorney general or state police website where you live.

Another good source of information is a website called USAcarry.com. They answer questions on reciprocity, no-carry zones, use of deadly force, firearm transportation and much more. This is especially handy if you're traveling through several states on a given trip. They also have many articles related to concealed carry. However, anything you find on the internet should be taken with a grain of salt and verified with other reliable sources.

> Be legally and morally justified, but also be wise.

NOTE: There is no substitute for an excellent attorney who is fluent with the laws on deadly force in your jurisdiction.

Stand Your Ground Laws

In some states you are required to retreat from a deadly threat if you can safely do so. In other states you are not. This is called "Stand your ground." I won't list these "Stand your ground" states because they are constantly changing. Your best bet is to do the research yourself and find out what the laws of your state are.

But another consideration is this. There are two questions to ask:

1. Are you legally justified in using deadly force? I've just

spent many pages going over that question.

2. Are you wise in using deadly force? Using deadly force can have certain rewards and consequences. If improperly applied, you can go to prison, get shot, get sued, etc. If properly applied you can save the life of yourself or another innocent person.

> When you carry, always be polite. Never argue or fight.

My final word of advice to you is this. Be very careful when deciding to use deadly force. It is a life-changing event. You and other people are going to live or die based on decisions you make. So take the time to get educated about the laws of deadly force in your jurisdiction.

Be polite

Above all, when you decide to strap on that firearm, you should become the most polite person on the planet. If you're walking down the sidewalk and you accidently brush shoulders with someone, they turn and swear at you, be quick to apologize and move on. It's not worth a gun fight. When you carry a gun, you should never argue or fight again. Angry words have a way of escalating into physical grappling and blows. Less than lethal force can quickly escalate into deadly force. Nothing good can come from verbal arguments or physical confrontations. The firearm is a tool of last resort and should only be used when you are legally justified and when there is no other way to save your life.

WARNING

Drinking alcohol and/or taking mind altering drugs is a very bad idea when carrying a firearm. Before you drink, always unload your gun, and lock it up so it is not accessible to you. Consult the laws of your jurisdiction for more details.

Pre-paid Self-defense Programs

There are many services out there offering you either a member-based program or an insurance policy just in case you get into legal trouble for using your firearm in self-defense. Currently, I have a membership in a company called *Firearms Legal Protection*, based in Dallas, Texas. I also have a policy with the *United States Concealed Carry Association* called *Self Defense Shield*. In times past, I've also used a service called *Armed Citizens Legal Defense Network*. All three are great services, and I can personally recommend them.

But it's important to understand that having self-defense legal protection is not a license to do stupid things with your firearm. Any company worth its salt will distance itself from stupidity. For example, you can have fire insurance on your house, but the policy becomes null and void if you set fire to your own dwelling.

I highly recommend you get some type of legal protection if you're going to be carrying concealed. I'll list the contact info for three services at the end of this chapter, along with places to go to get more detailed information on use of deadly force.

Firearms Legal Services

Here are the three legal services that I know and trust.

Firearms Legal Protection
www.firearmslegal.com/midwesttactical
Or call 844-357-9400

United States Concealed Carry Association
www.uscca.com
Or call 877-677-1919

Armed Citizens Legal Defense Network
www.armedcitizensnetwork.org
Or call 360-978-5200

Armed Citizens' Rules of Engagement

One of the best things I did after carrying concealed was to take a class taught by Massad Ayoob called *Armed Citizens' Rules of Engagement*. This 20-hour class gave me a very thorough understanding of when to shoot along with all the legal, moral and social implications of using deadly force. I highly recommend it. To find out more about this class and how to register, go to www.massadayoob.com.

Things to Remember

1. Firearms laws vary from state to state. Know the laws of your jurisdiction.

2. Your attacker must have the ability, opportunity and intent to kill or seriously injure you before you are availed the use of deadly force.

3. Before using deadly force you must honestly and reasonably believe you are in danger of being killed or seriously injured.

4. Serious bodily injury is any injury resulting in sutures, broken bones, permanent disfigurement or substantial loss of consciousness.

5. Consult a competent, certified attorney who knows the laws of your jurisdiction before deciding to carry concealed.

Chapter 11

In this chapter you will learn the following:

- How your brain makes decisions before a fire fight.
  - Visualization
  - The OODA Loop
  - Startle Response
  - Known and Unknown stimuli

11
If You Hesitate, You Die

DECIDING WHETHER OR NOT TO use deadly force in self-defense is a tricky proposition. If you decide too quickly, and your judgement is later called into question, then you could spend a lot of time and money tied up in the legal system, and maybe even end up incarcerated. However, if you hesitate in a situation that clearly necessitates the use of deadly force, then you could end up losing your life, and not even the best lawyer in the world can help you with that problem.

In this chapter we'll discuss how your brain makes decisions just prior to a firefight. The purpose is to help you train yourself to make the proper decision faster, without hesitation, in a way that saves your life and won't land you in prison.

Visualization Exercise

What is Visualization?

Visualization is a technique used in self-defense to "practice" putting yourself in harm's way without the accompanying danger normally associated with a deadly force confrontation. We know that all of self-defense is scenario-based and all scenarios are extremely fluid and dynamic. There are millions of different self-defense scenarios, and they change from moment to moment.

As a starting point, I highly recommend you read the article written by Dave Spaulding, international trainer and winner of the 2010 Law Officer Trainer of the Year. The article is titled "What Really Happens in a Gunfight," and you can find it quite easily online by searching for "Dave Spaulding What Really happens in a gunfight?"

Over the course of Dave's 25-year career in law enforcement, he's had the opportunity to interview approximately 200 gunfight survivors. Dave took notes and later analyzed the answers he'd collected. He asked the simple question: "What did these people have in common that helped them to survive the gunfight?" The results, though not scientific, are worthy of study and consideration.

The survivors tended to have a short startle-response time. Startle-response is the amount of time from the moment the deadly threat is perceived to the moment the person acted on the deadly threat. (I'll expand on this more when we discuss OODA Loop.) Some of the survivors routinely practiced the technique of visualization, and this practice shortened their startle-response time, allowing them to step into the fight quicker.

Practicing visualization is really quite simple. Wherever you are right now, reading this book, take a look around you. You are in a self-defense scenario every second of your life. If you are in a public library, surrounded by other people reading, with one clear exit to the room, then that is your scenario. Whatever your scenario, you simply begin by asking yourself this one question "What should I do if ..." and then you fill in the blank. "If a man walks in and starts stabbing people with a knife." or "if a group of men come in and start shooting in terrorist style." Your self-defense scenario is simply the details of the situation you are in right now. If you change one detail, then you change the scenario. If you change the scenario, then you change the outcome.

> Visualization is a kind of flight simulator for personal defense.

For example, if you are in a gas station and a man is holding a gun on the clerk, demanding money. That is one scenario. But scenarios are dependent on details, and details change quickly. All of a sudden, a police officer walks in to buy a cup of coffee. Suddenly, the officer and the criminal are thrust into a confrontation. The scenario has changed drastically in the twinkling of an eye, and there's going to be a firefight. Someone is going to start shooting and that should change your own response to the scenario.

You can change that up a million ways. Instead of a police

officer walking through the door, it could be a child running in with his mother close behind. You could have the store clerk refuse to hand over the money. Or the criminal could put the clerk down on her knees execution style. There is a limitless number of variations, and you should practice as many as you can.

> Practice visualization in your mind, but also physically on the range.

I practice visualization all the time and it drives my wife crazy. One time we were on a nice, romantic date having dinner. Like usual, I was seated facing the entrance, I'd already profiled everyone in the restaurant, and was busy making plans to respond to any and all threats. I'd already worked through one scenario and was busy formulating another. That's when I heard my wife say "Are you listening to me?"

I came back to reality and saw my wife looking me straight in the eye. I knew she'd been talking because I'd seen her lips moving. But I had no idea what she'd said because I was in the middle of a visualization scenario. I knew I was in trouble, but I've learned over the years, that the best thing to do in a situation like this is to tell the truth. So I said, "I'm sorry honey, I wasn't listening. I was thinking about something else."

Of course her next question was "What were you thinking about?" I should have seen that one coming because the moment we got married my brain was no longer my own. In her mind I became her property, so by extension, anything I was thinking also belonged to her. So I just spit it out.

"I'm sorry, honey. A man just walked in here with a shotgun and threatened to kill the cashier, but I pulled out my pistol and shot him several times in the upper chest. He's dead and everything's fine now."

My wife, God bless her, just nodded and then went on with her conversation as if nothing had happened. I'm going to keep her.

Once, after talking about visualization and situational awareness in class, a student raised his hands and announced to all present that he wasn't going to follow my advice. This is always a sticky situation, so I simply asked "And why is that?"

He went on to tell me that if he took my advice, that his life would no longer be worth living, that it would take all the joy out of his life if he had to walk around looking for threats all the time. I responded by saying, "You don't understand. This isn't an emotional thing I do. I'm not feeling anything at all while I'm scanning for threats or profiling. It's something I do automatically devoid of feeling and without thinking about it. It's a habit."

> Visualization is not emotional; it's a mental exercise.

I view the technique of visualization as a kind of flight simulator for personal defense. When you go to pilot's school, they don't just put you in an airplane and let you solo the first day. First, you do the book work, go to ground school, and then they put you in a flight simulator. They let you crash the simulator, and by making mistakes, you learn what you can get away with and what you can't. It's okay to crash and burn. That's how we learn, by making mistakes. After each visualization, you should ask yourself these questions:

- What did I do right?
- What did I do wrong?
- How would I do things differently next time?

Let's be honest here. We can't always be on the range shooting and training. Either we don't have the time, the range, the ammo, or a host of other things. However, visualization is one of the training techniques we can do in our everyday life to help prepare us for that deadly force confrontation. Along with watching training videos, reading books, dry firing and acting out reality-based simulations, visualization is just one more tool in your self-defense training arsenal, and you can practice it every day of your life.

What is the OODA loop?

"Time is the dominant parameter. The pilot who goes through the OODA cycle in the shortest time prevails because his opponent is caught responding to situations that have already changed."

– Harry Hillaker, F16 Chief Designer

One of the things I do as a co-host on the Frontlines of Freedom radio show is the tactical analysis for the Armed American Report. Colonel Denny Gillem, the primary host, starts by reading a self-defense scenario where an armed citizen protected himself with a firearm. I've been reading and studying those armed American reports for years, and was always amazed at how they typically all turn out the same way. That is, the bad guy is opposed with deadly force and he either flees or is shot by the armed citizen.

The typical situation is like this: The bad guy sticks a gun or knife into the good guy's face and demands something. The good guy reaches into his pocket or holster, draws a firearm and shoots the bad guy.

Question: The bad guy has all the advantages, so why doesn't he just shoot the good guy while the pistol is being drawn?

It never made sense to me until I stumbled across Colonel John Boyd's studies on response time and his famous OODA loop decision cycle.

Colonel John Richard Boyd was born in 1927 in Erie, Pennsylvania. He was a graduate of Iowa State University with a degree in Economics. Later, he earned an additional degree in Industrial Engineering from George Tech. He began his military career after graduating from high school and enlisting in the Army Air Corps in the year 1944. He served as a swimming instructor from 1945 to 1947 in occupied Japan. After that

> You can defeat a superior adversary if you make the element of surprise.

he went to college and eventually received his commission in the United States Air Force where he served as an officer from July 8, 1951, until his retirement on August 31, 1975.

Ironically enough, Boyd flew only 22 missions in the Korean War as a wingman, but never fired his guns or claimed a single aerial kill. Following the war, Boyd was assigned to the United States Air Force Weapons School, where he became head of the Academic Section and wrote the tactics manual for use there.

Boyd's primary contribution to the military was in his development of air combat theories. The theory he became most known for is called the OODA Loop. OODA Loop stands for:

- OBSERVE
- ORIENT
- DECIDE
- ACT

In reality, all of us experience the OODA Loop process hundreds of times in our everyday lives. Whenever something "happens" to us, we see what is occurring (OBSERVE) we then position ourself instinctively to react to it (ORIENT) then we make a determination as to what response is best in this situation (DECIDE) and finally we carry out that decision (ACT).

> We use the OODA Loop everyday without realizing it.

Now there are two primary ways this happens. We are always reacting to either a "known" stimulus or an "unknown" stimulus.

Known Stimulus - This is easy and is done in time measured in fractions of seconds. In the self-defense world we call this muscle memory, because we really don't have to spend much time thinking about it. We've been in this situation thousands of times before, so our mind and body simply "react." For example, you are driving your car down the road and you see the brake lights come on in the car in front of you. Without thinking, your foot immediately moves off the gas and presses on the brake.

Unknown Stimulus - This one isn't quite so easy, and it requires the full force of Boyd's OODA Loop decision-making process. An example of this could be "you are driving in town down a one-way street, when, all of a sudden, a car pulls out in front of you heading the wrong way. This is an unknown stimulus because it seldom, if ever, happens to you. So you go through the full OODA Loop of observing the car, orienting your hands on the steering wheel, deciding to turn the wheel, and then, finally, turning the wheel and avoiding the collision.

Thus, the OODA Loop for an unknown stimulus is measure in seconds instead of fractions of seconds. Let's translate this into the world of personal defense so you know how it applies in real life.

You are walking down the sidewalk of your hometown totally unaware of any danger, simply because you feel safe and this is a low-crime neighborhood. Suddenly, you see motion in your peripheral vision as a man steps out behind a hedge and points a gun at you. This is an unknown stimulus to you, because it's never happened before so you freeze. Your mind races to observe all that's happening to you, but the attacker quickly demands your wallet or he'll kill you. Because of the adrenaline dump into your bloodstream, your heartrate skyrockets, interrupting your brain's ability to think things through rationally and quickly. Because you are unprepared for this confrontation, you comply with the robber's demands, and you are at his mercy. Either he shoots you or he let's you go after getting your wallet.

> Rehearse your response in your mind AND on the shooting range.

This scenario happens to sheep everyday across the planet. But we don't want to be sheep, so we do it differently. Because we've practiced the technique of visualization, this is not an "unknown" stimulus to us, so our reaction and decision time is greatly reduced. In fact, there is no decision to make, because you've already made the decision hundreds of times in your own mind.

The robber steps out in front of you, points the gun, but, before he can utter a word, you turn and sprint away on a diagonal path to safety. He is left there with his mouth open, wondering what to do. You see, this is an "unknown" stimulus to him, and you've just screwed up his OODA Loop. In all likelihood, it will take him several seconds to decide what to

> You can choose to flee or you can choose to fight with confidence.

do and by then you'll be out of range and not worth his time. Is that a guarantee? No, of course not. There are no guarantees in a deadly confrontation. But the important thing is this: You did something immediately that he didn't expect. You forced your attacker to OBSERVE, ORIENT, DECIDE and ACT.

You have just forced the attacker to respond to a scenario that has already changed. He is one step behind you and that may be all the edge you need to prevail. But wait, you say, I'm 75 years old and I can't run very fast. That's okay. You can choose in your visualization exercise to stand and fight instead of running. You simply feign compliance by holding up both hands and begging for your life. "Yes sir, Please don't shoot me. I'll get my wallet. Then you slowly cant your gunside away from him and reach back to what he thinks is your wallet. Instead, you draw your pistol as you step off to one side and rapid fire into the upper chest area until the threat stops.

That's another way to handle it.

However, whichever scenario you choose, it should be rehearsed in your mind and also physically on the range. That's why training is so important.

I hope this chapter gives you new ideas into protecting yourself from a deadly threat. You don't have to be a helpless victim, regardless of your age, size, speed or strength. You can overcome all that using courage, training and the element of surprise.

Things to Remember

1. There are 2 types of stimuli: known and unknown.

2. Known stimulus allows you to react quickly.

3. Unknown stimulus may take seconds to respond.

4. Respond quickly and get out in front of your opponent, and screw up his OODA Loop.

5. Reality-based training helps train us to make quicker and better decisions in a real-life scenario.

Helpful Resources

"Boyd: The Fighter Pilot Who Changed the Art of War" written by Robert Coram, available on amazon. com

Read everything you can about the life and times of Colonel John Boyd. There is a lot of commentary online, and you can find it with a quick search on "Colonel John Boyd" or "OODA Loop."

Chapter 12

In this chapter you will learn the following:

- What happens to your mind and body during a firefight.
  - adrenaline dump
  - heart rate
  - tunnel vision
  - auditory exclusion
  - memory distortion
- Things you can do to train for the stress of a real-life firefight.

12

During the Shooting

AT THAT MOMENT IN TIME WHEN you suddenly realize you're about to die, unusual things start happening to your body. Many of these things can degrade your ability to fight for your life, so you need to know about them, and, more importantly, understand them and be able to fight through them.

Scenario

You're walking down the sidewalk in a city close to you. You had a business meeting, but now you're done and on your way back to your car. You're going home to your family where you'll fire up the grill, have dinner and then play catch with your son. So, that's what you're thinking of right now, and your situational awareness is out the window.

Suddenly, you see movement to your right, and a man

with a large knife and an evil smile steps out from behind the bushes and tells you to stop. At that moment in time, the following things are likely to happen to you. Let's go over them now and try to break them down and make them useful to you.

Adrenaline Dump

adrenaline (from merriam-webster.com)

noun | adren • a • line

a substance that is released in the body of a person who is feeling a strong emotion (such as excitement, fear, or anger) and that causes the heart to beat faster and gives the person more energy.

> **Increased heart-rate is a game-changer. Learn to fight under extreme stress.**

You've no doubt heard the stories of people who came across a car accident, and the driver was pinned beneath the car. The rescuer, overwhelmed with adrenaline, gained super-human strength and lifted the car off the driver. Just between you and me, I don't know that I believe all these stories, but I do know that adrenaline can do some pretty powerful things to the human body.

Increased heart rate: Once that adrenaline shoots into the bloodstream, the heart rate will skyrocket, and, depending on the individual, it can be a help or a hindrance.

60 to 80 beats per minute - This is a normal "at rest" heart rate. Anyone with a heart rate below 60 is considered to be an athlete in great shape.

115 beats per minute - At this point you lose fine motor skills. Fine motor skills are what you need to do things like press the slide release on your pistol or to pick up a quarter.

You can still draw and fire your pistol using only gross motor skills. Part of the reason this happens, is because your brain is anticipating a fight and some damage to your body. Because of this, it redirects blood flow from the extremities into the core of your body. This can leave your hands and fingers feeling numb and ice cold. That's why I use the overhand method to rack the slide instead of using the slide release mechanism (which is a fine motor skill.)

145 beats per minute - At this point you lose gross motor skills, making it difficult for you to draw your firearm and defend yourself.

175 beats per minute - At this point your body is useless to you. You are frozen in terror, unable to retreat, fight back or even think clearly.

200 beats per minute - Now, you are beyond useless. Your bowels evacuate and you no longer have control over any part of your body.

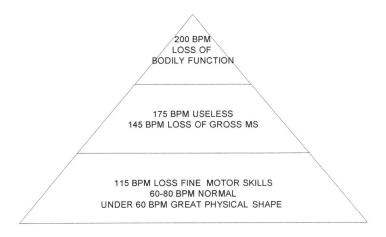

This is pretty serious stuff. But the important question is this: how can you overcome it and live?

It's not simple, but it can be done. It takes a lot of preparation and training. Whenever I get the chance, I always train under high stress. Rob Pincus has a drill called "Balance of Speed and Precision" where he uses special targets filled with different shapes, colors and numbers. He calls out a shape, color or number and you are expected to shoot that target in a short period of time. The drill forces you to act quickly, under stress, but also to think about what you're doing before you do it.

> Good training will desensitize you to stress, allowing you to better able make good hits.

The simple act of shooting in front of other people is also good practice. Most of us care about what others think of us, so shooting in front of others, even if we might bear the brunt of a little teasing can help sharpen us for a more stressful life-or-death situation.

Competition is a good thing, whether it's formal or just with your friends. Bowling pin shoots are good, IDPA competition, and anything else you can do safely under stress that will cause you to move and shoot is helpful.

One of the drills I do in my advanced classes is to create a great deal of stress by yelling commands from just a few feet away. This rattles people, and it throws them off even more when I change the commands and make them reassess the task. It also adds stress when you add a shot timer. When you're under the clock, everyone knows where you stand in the pecking order, and you struggle to come out on top. Even if you embarrass yourself, you still win because it makes you less stressed in a real-life shooting scenario.

Try to train in a fashion that forces you to incorporate the skills you're likely to need in a real gun fight. (Moving, shooting, making decisions, etc.) But please understand that you will never be able to re-create battlefield conditions in training.

WARNING: Shooting under stress can be dangerous. It can cause you to do unsafe things. Start out with just a little stress and then add to it in a safe manner. It's always best to train under the supervision of a competent professional instructor.

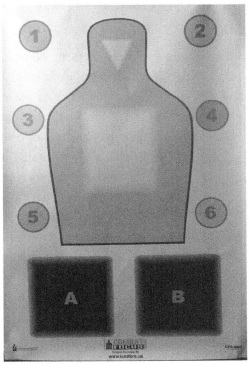

Balance of Speed and Precision targets by ICE Training, developed by Rob Pincus. I highly recommend them, and they can be purchased at www.icestore.us/targets.

Auditory Exclusion

In high stress situations, a part of your brain called the thalamus, filters out auditory data (sound). That doesn't mean your ear drums don't feel the sound waves or that they won't be damaged by the sound of gun shots, it simply means your brain won't be processing the auditory data. The brain does this because it's trying to simplify things for you, so you can concentrate on the threat. Auditory exclusion can result in either total or partial loss of hearing. The loss is temporary and will return when the stress lowers to a normal level.

Tunnel Vision

When that dynamic critical incident occurs, and your heartrate skyrockets, you may also experience something called tunnel vision. There are two kinds of sensors in your eyes; they are called rods and cones. Rods are located around the edges of your eyes and are responsible for detecting motion. Cones are located in the center of your eyes and help you see things in greater detail.

> Learn to fight through all the physical changes that occur in your body.

Just as in auditory exclusion, where the thalamus filters out unnecessary auditory input, now the thalamus filters out non-critical visual input, which includes anything not in the center of our vision. (Increased visual acuity in the center of vision.) Any object in the center of our vision will be seen in greater detail, but our field of vision will be greatly decreased. That's why police and military, as well as civilians, are taught to break the tunnel vision by moving their head from side to side while scanning for additional threats.

Time Distortion

In a critical incident your sense of time can either speed up or slow down. The thalamus is feeding data to the brain at an increased rate, but another part of your brain, called the temporal lobe, is unable to process all this data, and that's what causes this feeling of time distortion. Law enforcement studies reveal that approximately 70 percent of officers report a slowing down of time, while about 20 percent report time speeding up.

There is no way to know beforehand which of these time distortions, if any, you'll experience, but if you keep your eye on the threat, and act in accordance with your muscle memory and training, then you'll be able to work through it.

> During a gun fight, your brain processes information abnormally.

Memory Distortions

Memory distortions and even false memories can occur during a time of great emotional stress. That's the primary reason your defense lawyer will tell you to shut up and call him and to never talk to police without a lawyer present. Most will recommend you not make any statements until 48 to 72 hours after the shooting incident.

NOTE

Another way to measure this is in sleep cycles. It takes 3 to 4 good sleep cycles for the body to process and clear the chemicals from your system.

They say this because the brain processes input differently

during high stress, and you can't rely on your memory to be accurate until a period of hours or even days after the stress goes away. This has been taught to police officers for many years.

In 2001 an article was published for the Journal of International Law Enforcement Instructors stating that within the first 24 hours after an officer involved shooting, the officer is likely to remember only 30 percent of the incident. After 48 hours they'll remember 50 percent, and after 72 hours they'll recall 75 percent of the incident.

False memories can even occur under extreme stress, where people swear they saw something happen, but later examination of the scene and the evidence prove the event didn't take place.

> **Reality-based training is essential in personal and family protection.**

Reality-based Training

I want you to understand that training on a traditional gun range, in a traditional manner, is just the starting point. We call this "square range training." While it's important to start training on the traditional range, it's equally important that you eventually move beyond it.

On the traditional range, we learn many of the basic gunfighting skills. For example, clearing malfunctions, reloading, drawing from the holster, not to mention basic marksmanship. All these things are foundational to the gun fighter. But, if you're serious about personal defense training, there will come a time when you're ready to move beyond the world of square-range training and into the world of reality-based training. This necessitates you get formal training by a competent reality-based training instructor.

Reality-based training incorporates real-life scenarios into your training, using tools like rubber guns and airsoft training pistols. Typically, gun fights do not occur on the gun range, and it's extremely limiting to train with live firearms on a traditional range. It just can't be done well because of safety concerns.

I've always encouraged people to train for the dynamic critical incident, that is, the thing that's most likely to happen to you in your everyday life. A good example of reality-based training would be the following:

Inside your own home, set up targets (cardboard boxes filled with soft towels) at locations where a home invasion is likely to occur. Begin in your master bedroom, armed with an airsoft pistol (using proper eye protection) and then move to the threat and engage it. This allows you to operate in a familiar environment, the place where you are most likely to engage a threat, that is, in your own home.

You can make this scenario even more real by using a friend to play the role of a home invader. Suddenly, the training has become more real because the target is now shooting back. Do this scenario at night, in the dark, using flashlights, and the training gets even more real. Just be careful you do it all safely. Make sure the house is empty and that proper safety rules and equipment are used.

ICE Training is a good place to start. Watch the videos on reality-based training shown on www.icetraining.us. Then read a book by Ken Murray called *Training at the Speed of Life*. Train hard and train safe.

Things to Remember

1. In a high-stress situation, your body will not function the way it usually does.

2. After a self-defense shooting, be careful what you tell police. Less is better. Call your lawyer as soon as possible.

3. Training under stress is a necessary part of personal protection.

4. The traditional gun range teaches us the basics of gun fighting.

5. Reality-based training teaches us how to implement those basics in a real-life scenario.

Helpful Resources

Training at the speed of Life, written by Ken Murray Read this book and learn how to set up your own reality-based training. Available at Amazon.com.

www.personaldefensenetwork.com - Subscribe to this website and get unlimited access to training films, classes and interviews from the world's top self-defense instructors.

www.realitybasedtraining.com - Subscribe to the RTBA newsletter. Learn about new training technologies and find a competent reality-based trainer near you.

Counter Ambush Concepts: Physics and Physiology, by Rob Pincus of ICE Training. This can be purchased and streamed online through the Personal Defense Network subscription or purchased as a 5-DVD set. This is online training, but certificate is awarded.

Chapter 13

In this chapter you will learn the following:

- What do I do if I have to use my gun to protect myself.
  - securing the scene
  - calling 911
  - talking with police
  - what are your rights?

13

After the Shooting

WE'VE ALREADY DETERMINED that all self-defense is scenario-based, and that all scenarios are extremely fluid and dynamic, changing from moment to moment. So here's a scenario.

You are driving your car and not paying close attention. You pull into the left turn lane without using your blinkers, and accidently cut another driver off. They honk their horn, but you drive on, not wishing to escalate the situation. You pull into the store parking lot and get out of your car. You didn't notice the driver of the car you cut off minutes earlier had followed you and parked behind your car. You watch as a large, angry man gets out of his car and advances toward you brandishing a tire iron over his head. He yells as he advances, "You dirty, rotten $%$*! You cut me off on purpose and now I'm going to kill you!"

You feel the rush of adrenaline pump into your bloodstream. You fight to control your heart rate as you instinctively back up. There is a cement wall behind you and a maniacal man threatening to kill you to your front. Because you've practiced the technique of visualization, you already know that this man has the ability to kill you with that steel bar. He certainly has the opportunity as he's only a few yards away and advancing quickly. His intentions are obvious because he's just verbally articulated them to you and anyone else in hearing distance.

> You've just killed a man. What do you do now?

As quickly as you can, you clear your jacket and draw your firearm. You point it at the advancing attacker and aim for the center of his upper chest. He sees the gun but he doesn't stop his attack. Seeing no other option, you fire five times into the center of exposed mass. He still reaches you and hits you with the tire iron which glances off your left cheek. The man goes down, tries to get up, but is unable to get back to his feet. You are pressed against the cement wall with your gun pointed down at his back. Your hands are shaking; they are ice cold, and you look up and see several people staring at you aghast at what just happened.

QUESTION: What do you do now?

1. Break your tunnel vision and scan for other threats. Is there anyone else in his car? Is he going to get back up? These are all things that you need to know. Check yourself for injuries and make sure you are physically safe and the threat is over.

2. If the immediate threat is over, then you need to secure your firearm. The police will be coming, and you should not appear to be a threat to them. I recommend you secure your gun in your vehicle.

IMPORTANT SAFETY TIP: Never stand over a dead body holding a gun as police arrive at a crime scene. Chances are all the responding police have been told is that a shooting has occurred and a man is down. If they see you with a gun, they will treat you as a threat. You may have auditory exclusion and not correctly hear their command to drop your weapon. If you turn toward police with a gun, they could very well shoot you multiple times.

3. Call the emergency dispatcher at 911 and report the incident. Be the first person to call, because this will posture you as "the good guy." (In general, criminals don't call 911 and ask for the police to come to the scene.) Bear in mind that dispatchers are trained to ask a lot of questions and gather as much information as possible. All your answers are being recorded and can be used against you in a court of law. You have survived the deadly threat but now you need to survive our criminal justice system. As such, tell the dispatcher just the basic facts. "My name is John Smith, I am wearing a red shirt. A man has been shot. Here is the address. Please send police and an ambulance right away."

> Tell the dispatcher and the police "Just the basic facts." Then ask for your lawyer.

LEGAL TIP

Your second call should be to your attorney or prepaid legal protection service, if you have time before police arrive.

CAUTION

Never alter a crime scene. Don't change anything. Don't move the body; don't pick up your empty brass. Don't move his car. You can be charged and convicted of a crime if you change the crime scene.

You've no doubt heard the story "If a man breaks into your house and you shoot him and he falls outside, you should drag his body back in." I can't tell you how many times my students have told me they've been given that advice. And oddly enough, many times it's been police officers who've told them this. Don't take the chance. However the shooting goes down, just live with those facts and, if some of your actions are questionable, you should have a very good lawyer.

> **You can go to prison if you alter the crime scene. Don't change anything.**

Keep in mind that modern forensics are very advanced and the crime scene technicians will be able to determine if you've altered anything.

4. The police arrive with drawn firearms and immediately take control of the crime scene with overwhelming force. You should appear non-threatening to them in all your interactions. They will approach you and ask for information. You should be cooperative in a prudent and discretionary manner. *What exactly does that look like?* Here's an example.

YOU - "Officer, I'm the one who made the call to dispatch."

POLICE - "What happened here?"

YOU - "The man on the ground said he was going to kill me and attacked me with a tire iron. I feared for my life, and the results are what you see. Then I called dispatch."

POLICE - "Where is your gun now?"

YOU - "It's on the front seat of my car."

Always stick with just the basic facts when answering questions to the police. Did you ever watch that detective show back in the sixties with Jack Webb and Harry Morgan? They were both detectives, and whenever someone got too wordy, Sergeant Joe Friday would always say, "Just the facts, Ma'am."

That's how you want to answer the police. You can cooperate without giving away too many of the details. Because, remember, you're not thinking clearly after that adrenaline dump and that life-altering experience. You are distraught and not thinking clearly.

> Know your rights, and take the Miranda Warning seriously.

5. Depending on the individual police officer, the situation and the jurisdiction, you may be handcuffed, arrested and put in jail. If this occurs, the police will read you your Miranda rights, sometimes called a Miranda Warning.

Miranda Rights

- You have the right to remain silent and refuse to answer questions.
- Anything you say may be used against you in a court of law.
- You have the right to consult an attorney before speaking to the police and to have an attorney present during questioning now or in the future.
- If you cannot afford an attorney, one will be appointed for you before any questioning if you

wish.

- If you decide to answer questions now without an attorney present, you will still have the right to stop answering at any time until you talk to an attorney.

- Do you understand your rights as I have explained them to you? Are you willing to answer my questions without an attorney present?

Your 1st call is to 911. Your 2nd call is to your lawyer.

Take the Miranda warning very seriously. You are now wearing handcuffs and are in the back of a police car. You'll notice there are no door handles on the inside. Just because you're innocent, doesn't guarantee you won't be convicted of a crime and serve prison time. When it comes to speaking to police after a self-defense shooting, "Less is best."

They aren't just kidding you when they say "Anything you say may be used against you in a court of law." It WILL be used against you. So give the officer just the basic facts, and then ask for your lawyer.

"Officer, I don't mean to be difficult, but I need my attorney present during any questioning."

NOTE

According to the United States Supreme Court, you must positively assert your right to counsel during questioning and your right to remain silent. Until you assert those rights, the police will continue to question you, and anything you say can be used against you in court.

If you have the misfortune of getting a responding officer who pushes you to talk more and is abrasive or insulting, don't take it personal. They are just doing their job. But right now, they see their job as gathering as much information as possible so they can write a report and pass it on to the prosecuting attorney. At this point in time, the police are not your friends; they are not your buddies or your therapist. Their role is investigatory, and you've just killed a man.

As the police investigate, they will operate from a position of suspicion. In court, you are presumed innocent until proven guilty, but on the streets, this is not the case. When the police assume your guilt, they pursue every possible angle he can possibly identify. Only after finding no evidence to support your guilt, will he declare that you are not a suspect.

> **Verbally invoke your right to an attorney as soon as possible.**

NOTE

Do not wait to be arrested and for your Miranda rights to be read. Assert your right to counsel and to remain silent right away. The police will immediately ask questions and it will continue throughout the course of their investigation. If you answer their questions, your answers, even though you have not yet been Mirandized, can be used in court as "excited utterances" and can be used against you in a court of law.

If you were wise enough to purchase a membership in prepaid legal protection, then you'll be given the opportunity to make a phone call. Call the number on your membership card, and they'll do the rest. But don't make it hard for your defense attorney by blabbing away and stating details that may or may not prove to be accurate.

The person who wrote your will or handled your last divorce is not the guy to call. You need an attorney who has successfully defended and won cases like yours already. Your lawyer must have a proven track record.

Please understand the seriousness of the situation and don't take it lightly. This is the rest of your life we're talking about here. You could lose your freedom, your marriage, and access to all the people you know and love.

I'll repeat the contact info for the legal protection services now simply because I believe it's that important.

Firearms Legal Services

Here are the three legal services that I know and trust.

Firearms Legal Protection
www.firearmslegal.com/midwesttactical
Or call 844-357-9400

United States Concealed Carry Association
www.uscca.com
Or call 877-677-1919

Armed Citizens Legal Defense Network
www.armedcitizensnetwork.org
Or call 360-978-5200

Things to Remember

1. Never alter a crime scene, even if you made a less than perfect decision to shoot.

2. Try to be the first to call 911. Tell them the address, your name and to send police and medical help.

3. Tell the responding police just the basic facts, and that you will answer other questions when your lawyer is present.

4. Hire the best lawyer you can afford, one who has a track record of winning self-defense cases.

5. Subscribing to a firearms legal service gives you a great deal of legal protection and is a very good idea.

Chapter 14

In this chapter you will learn the following:

- How to defend yourself after your prime
- The importance of staying in shape
- The strength of old age
- Dealing with loss of eyesight, speed, stamina and strength

14
When Gunfighters Get Old?

ABOUT SEVEN MONTHS AGO, FROM the date of this writing, I squatted down to pick up a fifty-pound bag of chicken feed. I bent my knees so I wouldn't hurt my back and I lifted the bag and threw it up onto my right shoulder. I felt something weird give way near my left hip and then excruciating pain. I pushed the sack of feed off my shoulder and let it drop on the ground. I quickly followed it to the grass. I couldn't stand, so I had to slowly crawl my way back into the house. That was the moment in my life when I began to feel my age. I was 58 years old.

This injury has caused me to make some changes in my personal defense plan. I've had to admit that I can't do the things I used to. In this chapter we'll explore how old age affects us all, and how we can still protect ourselves, despite the fact that we're no longer in our prime.

Loss of Speed and Mobility

Up until now, I've always been pretty fast, even at 59 years old. When I think of me running these days I'm reminded of a quote from the Lord of the Rings movie *The Two Towers*. The short-legged dwarf Gimli is trying to keep up with Legolas and Aragorn as they run for miles and miles without rest. Gimli says, struggling to breathe. "We dwarves are natural sprinters, very dangerous over short distances."

> **We must adapt to our fading physical abilities.**

I feel more like Gimli now. I could sprint a few yards to save my life, but, even then, my sprinting isn't as fast as it used to be. You've heard of the "Fight or Flight" reflex? When a person reaches a certain age, there is no more fight or flight, because you are no longer capable of outrunning a twenty-something attacker. You are forced to stand and fight.

Loss of eyesight

I remember two years ago I was taking a week-long Patrol Rifle Instructor course from a criminal justice center in my home state. We were firing AR15s out at 200 yards, and I was having trouble hitting the target. The instructor tried to help me out. It went something like this.

ME - Where did my shot hit?

HIM - Down by that rock.

ME - What rock?

HIM - The one two feet from the target at about seven o'clock.

ME - There's no rock there.

HIM - Okay, I think we found the problem,

What he meant to say was, "Skip, you're blind as a one-eyed bat in a snowstorm."

I can remember shooting my M16 at 18 years of age in the Marine Corps. I had no trouble hitting a silhouette at 500 yards. So, what changed? The simple answer is "I got old."

The degradation of my eyesight makes it difficult for me to see details in low light and also at longer distances. This greatly affects my ability to recognize a threat.

Low light is when I feel most vulnerable and when criminals are most likely to prey upon me. Here's an example of how this could impact me.

I'm walking out of Walmart at 9PM; it's dark outside and all I have is the light from the mercury bulbs overhead. I see a large man coming toward me. By his gait I can tell that he's young and in shape. There is something in his hand. It's long and about as big around as a knife. I go on full alert as he gets closer. I veer off to my right, but he changes course to follow me. When he gets about twenty feet away, I hold up my hand and yell "STOP!"

> Correct your eyesight whenever possible. You need your eyes.

The man hesitates and looks around as if confused. He takes another step forward. I clear my clothing and place my hand on my pistol. He stops again. Then I hear him say, "Skip, what the hell's wrong with you? Don't you recognize me?" At that moment I realize this is a former student of mine, but my eyesight just didn't see enough detail to make the connection. And the knife in his hand is a turkey baster that his wife wants him to return for a refund. I'm pretty sure a turkey baster, even in the most capable hands, does not constitute deadly force.

Now, that situation didn't happen - I just made it up, but that is a good example of what can happen as you age and your eyesight deteriorates. Threat identification is key in determining when you are legally justified in using deadly force. Good eyesight is also helpful when looking at a person's face to see what he's doing with his eyes. Is he looking at me? Is he smiling, frowning, scowling? All of these things are part of the big picture and help out with my gut instincts.

> You can defend yourself despite your old age and injuries.

Loss of Physical Strength and Stamina

I teach a class called "Stopping the Active Killer." And in this class I teach my students how to physically take down the bad guy with just bare hands. But these are normal people with very little training in hand-to-hand techniques. Let's face it, most of us aren't Ninjas. We're just people. But I want my students to realize that once they get into an all-out brawl, a fight to the death with bare hands, that it's not what they think it will be. They'll have between 10 and 30 seconds of their best strength and speed before things start to wane.

So I have them punch a body bag as fast and hard as they can while I run the timer and the rest of the class watches. Some people make it to only 10 seconds before they start to slow down. (Those are usually the smokers.) Most people make it to between 15 and 20 seconds before their punches lose force and become less frequent. The younger ones in their twenties can usually make it to 25 to 30 seconds. This knowledge should change how we train and how we fight.

Loss of Deterrence

I was at a store parking lot the other day when I saw an old man walking down the sidewalk. His back was hunched over so far that he was looking at the ground. His shoulders were slouched down and he was moving painfully slow. He was probably in his 80s or 90s. I felt sorry for him. It was painful just to watch him walk.

When the criminal stakes out the parking lot looking for victims, this is the man he's looking for: a quick, easy target. Remember the saying "Look like sheep, you'll be eaten by wolves." Well, you can do that only so long and then age catches up with you. There will come a point in your life when you no longer have the deterrent capability to ward off threats. This is inevitable, and, indeed, a best-case scenario. It means you've lived a long and happy life.

> Your physical appearance is no longer as capable of deterring.

But sooner or later you'll have to recognize that you are the preferred victim of wolves and take appropriate precautions.

The Solution

Okay, so you might be saying right now, "Skip, shut up with the old man stuff. I know I'm getting older and I don't want to be reminded of it. I understand, believe me I do. But now we have to look at possible things we can change in order to lessen your vulnerability and make you less tempting to the wolf.

Loss of Speed and Mobility

Okay, so you can't run that 100-yard dash in 10 seconds flat anymore. Maybe you have a hip replacement and you can't run at all. About a third of my students these days are 50 and older, so lets go over some possible changes you can make to help you survive an altercation.

1. If you can't run, you have to stand and fight. Practice more on the range shooting from within 10 feet. Make your draw smooth and perfect. Remember, slow is smooth and smooth is fast.

2. Get nasty when it comes to close-in fighting. Go for the eyes, always go for the eyes. Get some close quarters combat training. You won't be able to do all of it, but find something you can do and perfect it. (Hint: ink pens aren't just for writing. Google "Security self defense pen.") Other common items you can become proficient with are canes and umbrellas. They are effective and have a longer reach.

> You are too old to run away. You have to stand and fight!

Loss of Eyesight

For most of us, this is the easiest problem to fix. Let your pride go and get some glasses. This was hard for me because I didn't want to admit I was getting old. Pride is a fault when it gets you killed. When shooting from contact distances, eyesight isn't as important. However, when it comes to identifying the threat, that's when you'll need clearer eyesight to see their eyes and the looks on people's faces as well as the objects in their hands.

You may have to make some changes in your lifestyle. Try to do your shopping during daylight hours, when criminals are sleeping off the night before and when there are others out and about as a deterrent and to help you if things get nasty.

Don't be afraid to ask a son or daughter or even a grand child to come with you and be your eyes.

Loss of Physical Strength and Stamina

There is no easy fix for loss of strength and stamina. It's a natural result of old age. You're going to lose muscle mass. But it's important to note that many people become old before their time. Let's face it, most of America is already out of shape whether they're young or old. Kids sit in front of video games all day and older folks sit in front of the television. My advice to you is to continue to do physical workouts. In fact, you should ramp it up a bit.

> You can be in shape at any age. But not if you surrender.

CAUTION

Don't kill yourself. If you're already out of shape, then start out very slowly and gradually get back in shape. Most people fail in this because they start out very ambitious but can't maintain the pace. Get professional help if needed.

You will never be what you were at age twenty, but you can be in good shape for your age. I write this fully understanding that you may not be able to jog or even walk because of degenerative illnesses. That's okay. If your legs are bad, then work out your arms. Just do the best you can with what you have, but always work to improve what you have.

One of the best things you can do is lose some weight. I'm

going to put that in all caps so you understand how important it is. LOSE SOME WEIGHT! That means a lifestyle change. Along with the exercise, you have to change what you eat. I see some people in my classes who can't run or even walk fast, but if they lost 50 pounds they would do much better.

When I was a much younger man, I used to look at overweight people and chuckle to myself. Then I'd have a Mountain Dew and a couple Twinkies for lunch and go on with my life. That caught up with me. I have severely cut back on my Mountain Dew and Mocha Frappuccino consumption. This was hard for me to do, but I did it and still struggle with it. Find a lifestyle that works for you and make it happen.

Loss of Deterrence

This is a tough one. You can't make a 75-year-old man look like he's twenty. It just can't be done. But do the best you can. If you're in the best shape you can be, then you can be a better deterrent than if you're overweight and out of breath after walking up a flight of stairs.

Excess weight causes a host of other physical problems.

My advice is to don't look your age. I firmly believe that people in America age much too quickly. And it's because they give up on the inside. At a certain age your body slows down; cells die, metabolism slows down, you gain weight quicker and it seems harder to lose it once you have it. This can be very discouraging. I began understanding this around age 45. Then when I herniated a disk in my back, it took on a whole new meaning. The important thing is to never give up trying to get in shape; never stop trying to lose weight. Once you give up the game is over. In that regard the battle for deterrence is as much mental as it is physical.

I've noticed the people who still feel young on the inside also look young on the outside, despite their age. If you can maintain that warrior spirit that says "I will never give up! I will never lose!" then you'll appear younger on the outside and feel younger on the inside. I've seen this time and again in self-defense situations where younger attackers were subdued and conquered by people in their 70s, 80s and even 90s.

Bottom line is once you give up on the inside your body will quickly follow suit. Stay active with other people your age and even with younger people. Travel in packs when you're in public. There is indeed safety in numbers. Always carry your gun as well as other weapons lethal or otherwise.

One of the biggest advantages you have as an older person is your appearance. Quite often a person's greatest weakness is also his greatest strength. The fact that you look old, weak and frail is also an advantage to you. Why? Because the wolf will look at you and think you're an easy mark. In truth, you're not defenseless. You have a lifetime of experience and wisdom as well as that warrior spirit that still burns inside you.

> The battle for self-defense during old age is both mental and physical.

Always remember that if you have the element of surprise you can overcome superior numbers and superior firepower. And you are the last person in the world the wolf expects to fight back. Plus, you have a gun. You can not only fight back, but you can also kill him and make sure no one else is hurt by him.

Let's look at it another way. A young man in his prime can shoot an attacker and the jury will think "Why didn't he run away" or "Why didn't he fight him with his fists? He didn't have to kill him." The jury will not look at you in the same way. They will see a defenseless old person who is lucky to even be alive.

In truth you are less of a deterrent than ever before in your life, but that doesn't make you defenseless. It just means you have different strengths and weaknesses. You should learn to rely on your strengths and avoid your weaknesses.

Things to Remember

1. Correct your eyesight if possible.

2. Lose the extra weight. It causes more problems than it's worth.

3. Start an exercise program and stick with it. Remember to start out slow.

4. Maintain your situational awareness and your warrior mindset. It's more important now than ever before.

5. Carry your gun always, and become proficient with close quarters combat.

6. Check into other weapons such as knives, umbrellas and canes. Become proficient in their use.

In Conclusion

IT'S GETTING SCARY OUT THERE. I'M not talking about just the hood, the big cities, or even third-world countries but about civilization in general. People everywhere are looking around them, watching the news and saying "Something feels different than before." The whole world is running scared – especially here in America. We're not used to third-world antics here. We expect to be kept safe by police as we shop in the mall, peacefully watch a movie or maybe even worship in church. We go to bed expecting a good night's sleep, free from worry or fear.

But something in society has changed.

I'm reminded of these lines from the opening of *The Lord of the Rings*.

> "The world is changed.
> I feel it in the water.
> I feel it in the earth.
> I smell it in the air.
> Much that once was ... is lost.
> For none now live who remember it."

Our borders are nonexistent. Terrorism is on the rise. We are trillions of dollars in debt, and many experts say it's only a matter of time before our economy crashes. Our leaders keep telling us that things are getting better, but ... the world is changed. I can feel it. Is anarchy about to be loosed upon the earth?

All of us prepare in our own ways, as best we can, but most of us don't know how to do it. How does one even prepare for societal collapse, something that's never happened to us? We have no concept of it. But, if truth be told, societal collapse has always been the rule and not the exception. Look back through history and ask yourself: Where are the ancient Babylonians, the Egyptians, the Greeks, the Romans, the British Empire? Gone. All gone. Civilizations come and go, and one culture is built upon the ash heap of another. And life goes on, not as it was, but still, it goes on.

And now, once again, history is ripe for change. America, the greatest country ever to grace the planet, is in severe decline; some would say a downward spiral into graft and corruption, and I tend to agree with them. It's possible that we'll not pull out of this spiral. If so all that remains is preparation for change. Those who prepare can survive. Those who are strong will adapt and flourish. But let there be no mistake about it. In the near future, many who now read my words may not survive the transition.

My concealed carry class attendance has always been a cultural barometer for me. Back in 2000 I was lucky to field a class of five people. Then came nine-eleven and middle-aged men armed themselves and my classes flourished. Then it tapered off gradually until Barack Obama won the presidency. Then it surged again. And the surge continues. But this time it's different. It's not just middle-aged men who are arming – it's women as well. And, for the first time, twenty-somethings are getting armed and trained to face whatever unknown threat is out there.

As a firearms instructor, I find the change bittersweet. I love that people everywhere are transitioning to protectors and defenders, but … it saddens me that the world has degraded to such a point they feel the need to arm themselves. The world is changed. The change is permanent. The change is irrevocable.

In years past people would take the basic concealed carry class, get a permit from the government, buy a gun, and then rest in the illusion of safety. That too is changing. For many people the illusion is no longer sufficient. If society implodes, then illusion will not suffice. Most people who take my 8-hour basic concealed carry class walk away with enough knowledge and skill to keep from hurting themselves or innocent people around them. In an average mugging, if nothing goes wrong, and with a little luck; they'll probably survive. But if anything beyond that happens ... God help them. And that's why more people are taking advanced training. If a man stands up in church and starts shooting, they now realize their present skill set isn't enough. Training enhances survival. How do I take out a suicidal man wielding an AK-47? How do I engage a terrorist cell? How do I survive getting caught in a race riot?

Average Americans are now thinking about such things, because they understand and feel it in their bones. The change is imminent; the change is visceral; and the change is epic and profound. In terms of personal and family protection; it's come to Jesus time – now or never. Gaining, mastering and maintaining personal defense skills takes time, effort, planning and money. If you haven't already started, best do so now before it's too late.

Because the change on the horizon is real, the illusion of self-defense will no longer serve you. When illusion battles reality, flesh and blood and bullet will always win. If you want to step up your game, and move to the next level, call someone like me and we'll help. But you best hurry ... before we are cast into shadow.

– Skip Coryell
www.mwtac.com

Appendix 1

This appendix contains a series of tests that serve to rein-force the lessons taught in this book. It can also be used by instructors to test the knowledge of their students

The answers are given in Appendix 2

Test

Chapter 1 - What is Civilian Combat?

1.   The police will always be there in time to protect you.

> ***True***
> ***False***

2.   It is your responsibility to protect yourself and the ones you love.

> ***True***
> ***False***

Chapter 2 - A Nation of Sheep

3.   There are 2 kinds of people: sheep and wolves.

> ***True***
> ***False***

4.   A great deal of personal protection occurs in your mind. It's a lifestyle – a mindset.

> ***True***
> ***False***

Chapter 3 - Anyone Can Kill

5.   During a gun fight you will have plenty of time to decide if you are capable of using deadly force.

> ***True***
> ***False***

6.   All of self defense is scenario based, and all scenarios can change from moment to moment.

True
False

Chapter 4 - Anyone Can be Killed

7.   The gun is not a magic talisman that wards away evil. It's just a tool. Master the tool, and you'll enhance your chances of prevailing in a gunfight.

True
False

8.   You are likely to receive plenty of advanced warning before a violent encounter.

True
False

Chapter 5 - Never Give Up!

9.   When you can safely disengage, retreat is usually the wisest option.

True
False

10.   When you cannot disengage, fight with all you've got.

True
False

Chapter 6 - Rules for Gun Handling

11.   Once you're sure the gun is unloaded, it's okay to point it at someone.

   True
   False

12.   You should never give access of your guns to untrustworthy people.

   True
   False

13.   Never allow children to shoot guns without competent supervision.

   True
   False

14.   Always keep your guns locked up until you are ready to use them.

   True
   False

Chapter 7 - Choosing the Gun

15.   It is a good idea to shoot the type of gun you want prior to purchase.

   True
   False

16.   Make sure you can operate the gun, e.g., rack the slide, press the trigger, and engage safety mechanisms

prior to buying.

> *True*
> *False*

17.   You should shoot the highest caliber gun on the market, regardless of recoil.

> *True*
> *False*

Chapter 8 - The Method of Carry

18.   All holsters are simple. It doesn't matter which one you buy.

> *True*
> *False*

19.   There are 2 types of carry: on-body carry and off-body carry.

> *True*
> *False*

20.   If you carry your gun in a purse, you should be certain the purse is always under your control.

> *True*
> *False*

21.   Any holster which does not protect the trigger from accidental discharge is unsafe.

> *True*
> *False*

Chapter 9 - Stopping the Threat

22.   In most cases, shoot for the center of the upper chest area. This is the most forgiving, high-percentage shot.

True
False

23.   When you are using sighted fire, always focus on the rear sight.

True
False

24.   You should always shoot for the head as it stops your attacker 95% of the time.

True
False

25.   In a hydraulic stop, the body runs low on blood and your attacker passes out from oxygen loss to the brain.

True
False

Chapter 10 - When Can I Shoot?

26.   Firearms laws are the same from state to state. If you know one, you know them all.

True
False

27.   Your attacker must have the ability, opportunity and intent to kill or seriously injure you before you are availed

the use of deadly force.

True
False

28.   Before using deadly force you must honestly and reasonably believe you are in danger of being killed or seriously injured.

True
False

29.   Serious bodily injury is any injury resulting in sutures, broken bones, permanent disfigurement or substantial loss of consciousness.

True
False

30.   It is not necessary to have a lawyer after you've been arrested. Talk to the police and answer all their questions as thoroughly as possible.

True
False

Chapter 11- During the Shooting

31.   During the extreme stress of a gunfight, you are likely to lose fine motor skills.

True
False

32.   Training under stress can help you fight more effec-

tively in a real-life gun fight.

> *True*
> *False*

33.   At 150 beats per minute, you will lose control of all bodily functions.

> *True*
> *False*

Chapter 12 - If you Hesitate, You Die

34.   Colonel John Boyd's OODA Loop stands for Observe, Occupy, Deflect and Act.

> *True*
> *False*

35.   Reality-based training helps train us to make quicker and better decisions in a real-life scenario.

> *True*
> *False*

Chapter 13 - After the Shooting

36.   It's okay to alter a crime scene, as long as you are innocent.

> *True*
> *False*

37.   After you shoot someone in self-defense, try to be the first to call 911. Tell them the address, your name and to send police and medical help.

True
False

38.   Tell the responding police just the basic facts, and that you will answer other questions when your lawyer is present.

True
False

Chapter 14 - When Gunfighters Get Old

39.   As you age, your ability to flee from an attacker lessons.

True
False

40.   Once you become old, you should automatically comply with your attacker since you have little hope of defending yourself.

True
False

Appendix 2

The answer to the student test in Appendix 1 can be found at this web link.

http://www.mwtac.com/civilian-combat-info.html

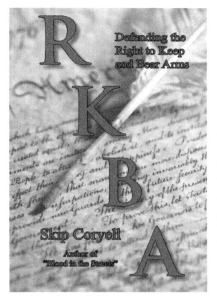

Columbine and Virginia Tech were not good omens. The victims there were unarmed sheep, who hid beneath desks and chairs, simply cowering as they died. They said "Baa" as they were being slaughtered. Something basic to our society has to change. It's time to stand and fight while we still can. And if our politicians tell us we can't protect our children in a daycare center, a post office, or a church, then we show them the door. We vote them out. We recall them. We take out the trash! That's the attitude that America was founded on. Somewhere along the timeline, America has lost it's way, we've lost our instinct for survival; it's no longer "fight or flight"; it's just plain "cower and die"!

Don't cower in the face of crime! Read this book and make your stand. That's one of the themes in Skip Coryell's new book *RKBA: Defending the Right to Keep and Bear Arms*.

FRONTLINES OF FREEDOM RADIO

You can listen to author and co-host Skip Coryell on one of your local stations on the number 1 military talk show in America. Frontlines of Freedom is syndicated on over 100 stations. You can also podcast it at www. frontlinesoffreedom.com.

Books by Skip Coryell

We Hold These Truths
Bond of Unseen Blood
Church and State
Blood in the Streets
Laughter and Tears
RKBA: Defending the Right to Keep and Bear Arms
Stalking Natalie
The God Virus
The Shadow Militia
The Saracen Tide
Civilian Combat: The Concealed Carry Book

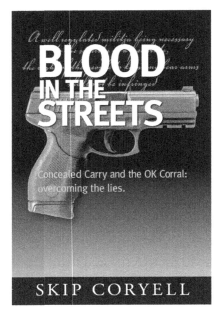

The world is smaller than it used to be. We all live closer together, brushing elbows more often, getting on each other's nerves, causing confrontation to happen more and more. It is inevitable. Moral relativism has permeated our society, telling us that there is no right and wrong, no good or bad, that each person must decide what is right in his own mind. (Of course, in the mind of a paranoid schizophrenic, the right thing to do is to kill your brother with a knife.) God, the ultimate authority on right and wrong, is being systematically removed from our schools, the courts, and from the legislative process. As always, cause and effect reign supreme. Without God, there is no accountability and no ultimate punishment after death. The deterrence that once held the wolves at bay has been removed and it's Katie bar the door. Things aren't right with America or the world, and that's why I carry a gun; that's why I train; that's why I train others. The post-nine-eleven society of our beloved country is different than the land of our fathers. Sometimes it seems like the world has gone crazy. How shall we then live? How shall we then survive?

Made in the USA
Middletown, DE
13 September 2021

48206828R00136